CASTRO'S COLONY

Castro's Colony

Empresario Development in Texas,

1842–1865

By

BOBBY D. WEAVER

Texas A&M University Press
COLLEGE STATION

Library of Congress Cataloging in Publication Data

Weaver, Bobby.
   Castro's colony.

   Bibliography: p.
   Includes index.
   1. Texas—History—Republic, 1836–1846—Case
studies. 2. Texas—History—1846–1950—Case studies.
3. Land settlement—Texas—History—19th century—
Case studies. 4. Castro, Henri, 1786–1865. 5. Castroville (Tex.)—History. I. Title.
F390.W37 1985   976.4'04   84-40139
ISBN 0-89096-210-3

Manufactured in the United States of America
FIRST EDITION

For Dianna

Contents

List of Illustrations   ix
Preface   xi
Acknowledgments   xv

CHAPTER

1. The Empresarios of 1842   3
2. The Project Begins   23
3. A Town is Founded   40
4. The Reorganization   57
5. Settling the Grant, 1845−47   73
6. The Colonists: Adapting to a New Life   89
7. The Land: Distributing the Grant Property   109
8. Settling In: 1850−65   124
   Bibliography   141
   Index   155

Illustrations

Frontispiece: Henri Castro at about the time of the start of his colonization project. (Courtesy Barker Texas History Center, University of Texas at Austin)

following p. 80

Henri Castro about the time of the Civil War
Land certificate for a Castro Colony grant
First page of a colonization contract
Castroville in the late 1840s
The Groff family of Medina County
St. Louis Catholic Church
The 1870 St. Louis Catholic Church and Moye Academy
Bishop Jean Marie Odin
Father Claude Marie Dubuis
Castroville about 1850
Landmark Inn, Castroville
Floor plan of the Landmark Inn
Theodore Gentilz

MAPS

Republic of Texas Empresario Land Grants, 1841–42   20
Castro's Colony: Towns Founded   82
Castro's Colony: Landforms and Previously Granted
    Lands   114
Castro's Colony: Lands Granted to Castro and His
    Colonists   118

Preface

THERE are many ways to explain American history. Some have described it as the saga of powerful men struggling to mold the nation in the form they deemed best. Others have seen it as the massive interaction of groups whose pursuit of varied interests developed the institutions of the country. Still others have viewed it as a reaction to environmental forces that channeled economic and social forces in certain directions. Yet a most important fact in American history is that the nation began as a vast sparsely settled land mass whose history developed as the population increased. Thus the settlement process has been a critical aspect of American history.

From the time of the sixteenth-century European settlement in North and South America, private agents received compensation to aid imperial policy. The British proprietorship, the Dutch patroonship, the French seigneury, and the Portuguese captaincy all represented institutions used for this purpose. The problem of settling and governing vast areas of land lay beyond the financial means of the European nations. So they contracted with private individuals to do the job. All of these colonization concepts included transportation of colonists to the new world.[1]

After the United States became independent from England, the new nation began to develop a land policy that

---

[1]Charles Gibson, *Spain in America*, 48–67; Wallace Notestein, *The English People on the Eve of Colonization*, 250–66; Wesley Frank Craven, *The Colonies in Transition*, 68–103.

xi

varied somewhat from the private contracting system of the
European powers. The new nation rewarded military service
and other assistance to the country with land donations and
began to sell portions of the public domain. This policy was
designed to settle the frontier as rapidly as possible while at
the same time furnishing most of the financial support for
the new nation. By the 1830s, during Andrew Jackson's administration, most of the Mississippi Valley was settled and
there was actually a surplus in the United States treasury.

By around 1800 the Spanish empire had reached its
northern limits in Texas and New Mexico. The remote location of the region combined with its lack of such wealth-
producing resources as mines made it an unpopular settlement area. Despite repeated efforts to colonize the region,
the nineteenth century dawned with fewer than 5,000 Spanish citizens in Texas. The Spanish government looked in vain
for a means to make the area secure, particularly after several filibustering expeditions entered the region from the
territory of the rapidly expanding United States. Some officials believed that encouraging United States citizens to
colonize Texas and become Spanish citizens might discourage filibusters and make the area secure for Spain.[2]

The first contract to introduce Anglos into Texas was
made in 1821. It was termed an empresario land grant (after
a Spanish term for one who undertakes an enterprise), and it
was issued to Stephen F. Austin to settle 300 Anglo colonists
on a grant in excess of 200,000 acres. In 1821 Mexico became independent from Spain, so Austin, whose father received the grant from Spain the previous year, persuaded the
Mexican government to validate the contract.[3]

Ultimately Austin and numerous other individuals received empresario contracts. At least nine of those empresarios actually introduced settlers into Texas. A flood of people

[2]Odie B. Faulk, "The Penetration of Foreigners and Foreign Ideas into Spanish East Texas, 1793–1810," *East Texas Historical Journal* 2 (1964): 87–94; for a good
overview of the filibustering expeditions see Warren Harris Gaylord, *The Sword Was
Their Passport.*

[3]Eugene C. Barker, *The Life of Stephen F. Austin, Founder of Texas, 1793–1836,*
23–79.

poured into the region which by 1830 contained more than 20,000 new citizens. The tremendous success of the empresario program alarmed Mexican officials who stopped the influx from the United States by a law passed in 1830. They feared that the new settlers, who outnumbered the original Mexican citizens by a ratio of four to one, would create unrest in the province.[4]

The fear of conflict in Texas evidently was justified. Various differences between Anglo Texans and government officials combined with the general political unrest in Mexico to produce a revolution. Fighting, which began in late 1835, led to independence for Texas in the spring of 1836. The citizens selected as their leaders former United States citizens who drew upon the long tradition of English and United States land policy to help stabilize their new nation.[5]

The Republic of Texas remained an independent nation from 1836 until it became a part of the United States in 1845. The new nation concerned itself with finance, defense, foreign relations, and the problem of populating its vast public domain. The last problem impinged directly on all the others because the nation depended upon population and land sales to support the government.

The Republic of Texas tried several methods of land distribution to stimulate population growth. The leaders of the republic gave land donations to veterans and others who had helped the republic as well as offering free public lands to attract settlers to Texas. Then they attempted to sell the public domain in imitation of United States land policy. Finally they settled on a contract system popularly called an empresario system despite the fact that Texas was no longer a Mexican possession. The new land-grant system was very similar to the one that originally had attracted a large population to Texas.[6]

[4] Eugene C. Barker, "Land Speculation as a Cause of the Texas Revolution," *Southwestern Historical Quarterly* 10 (1906): 76–95; Mary Virginia Henderson, "Minor Empresario Contracts for the Colonization of Texas, 1825–1834," *Southwestern Historical Quarterly* 31 (1927): 295–324; 32 (1928): 1–28.
[5] Barker, *Stephen F. Austin*, 427–46.
[6] Elgin Williams, *The Antimating Pursuits of Speculation*, 89–100.

xivPreface

Although most of the empresario contracts made by the Republic of Texas were canceled within a short time, they attracted a considerable influx of settlers and the publicity they generated created a continuing movement to the area, particularly from Europe. The establishment of a colony under such a contract by Henri Castro presents an excellent case study of the process by which the empresario system developed, how it operated, the results it achieved, and the impact it had on Texas.

Two book-length treatments of Castro's colony exist. The first, an unpublished 1928 University of Texas master's thesis by Audrey Goldthorpe entitled "Castro's Colony," presents an overly favorable view of Henri Castro, while giving only a cursory examination of the colony. Somewhat later, in 1934, Julia Nott Waugh published *Castroville and Henry Castro, Empresario*. The Waugh book is somewhat more perceptive, but its focus is on Castroville. Both of these books fail to place the colony within the historical perspective of Texas history, nor do they present an adequate study of the operation of the colony.

The study presented here proposes to tell the story of Castro's colony in considerable detail. First it describes the colony's relationship to Texas. Then it gives a detailed study of the way Castro recruited settlers and his land-distribution arrangement as well as the origins of the colonists and how they adjusted to the rigors of frontier life. Finally, it compares Castro's colony to other empresario projects under the auspices of the republic and assesses its importance in relation to the early history of Texas.

Acknowledgments

I cannot thank all those who helped me produce this work, but some individuals must be mentioned. The idea of writing about Henri Castro was first suggested to me by Dr. Seymour V. Connor in a seminar at Texas Tech University. That idea started becoming a reality when James Menke of San Antonio offered the use of his files on Castro's colony. Menke's help and advice during the research phase of the project provided insights that only someone with years of exposure to a subject can give. Without his support I would long ago have abandoned the project.

The suggestions of my doctoral committee including Dr. John Wunder, Dr. Dan Flores, Dr. Robert Hayes, Dr. Otto Nelson, and Dr. Evelyn Montgomery helped me over some of the rough spots. My chairman, Dr. Alwyn Barr, was extremely patient with my halting prose. I learned much from him and I owe him much.

I hope this study justifies the support I have received from all these individuals.

CASTRO'S COLONY

CHAPTER I

The Empresarios of 1842

LAND grants have played an important part in the history of Texas. The Spanish government consistently used land grants as an inducement to settle its northern boundary. Later the Mexican government used the same process when it issued empresario contracts to Stephen F. Austin and others to settle in Texas. Thus the Republic of Texas had a long-standing precedent for using grants to help populate and finance the new nation. Although this process remained in the minds of Texas leaders, they did not institute a large-scale empresario system until 1842.

As the year 1842 began, the Republic of Texas neared the end of its sixth year of existence, and things were not going well. Independence, so spectacularly gained at San Jacinto in April of 1836, had not been followed by the expected prosperity. Economic stagnation rather than prosperity seemed more the rule in a republic struggling with numerous problems, most of which centered around economic instability.

Unfortunately, the republic came into being just as the financial panic of 1837 began. In the following years the business community in the United States faced an overwhelming stagnation of credit and a flood of paper money that became worthless almost as soon as it was issued. The same phenomenon gripped Texas, where it was more severe and lasted longer than in the United States. This critical situation made it impossible for the new nation to assume any semblance of economic solvency.[1]

As one of its first remedies for the financial problem the republic issued paper money. In late 1837 and on into 1838 it circulated interest-bearing notes. These very quickly depreciated to 50 percent of their face value. Then between 1839 and 1841 the Lamar administration, which was incurring heavy expenses, increased the amount of Republic of Texas currency in circulation from $800,000 to $2,500,000 by issuing the "red backs." This particular currency dropped rapidly to eight cents on the dollar and by 1842 both the interest-bearing notes and the red backs listed at only 2 percent of face value. The situation deteriorated to the point that in January of 1842 the republic refused to accept either issue in payment of duties or taxes. Later that same year the Houston administration issued the "exchequer" currency, which, although it dropped to a low of 30 cents on the dollar, maintained a fairly stable position and rose to almost face value as 1845 and annexation neared.[2]

Another attempt to stabilize the republic's financial position was made through the sale of bonds. The Texas First Congress authorized the president to negotiate a loan not to exceed $5 million through the sale of interest-bearing bonds. Attempts to place these bonds on the United States market met with a notable lack of success, primarily because of the tight money situation engendered by the 1837 financial panic. Finally in the fall of 1839 part of the bonds were purchased by the Pennsylvania Bank of the United States. Encouraged by this beginning, one of the loan commissioners, Gen. James Hamilton, went to Europe to try to negotiate for the sale of the balance of the loan.[3]

Hamilton felt that the financial climate in Europe would be more favorable because the panic was less severe there. At

[1] William Ransom Hogan, *The Texas Republic*, 81–100.

[2] Anson Jones, *Memoranda and Official Correspondence Relating to the Republic of Texas, Its History and Annexation*, 24, 59.

[3] H. P. N. Gammel, *The Laws of Texas, 1822–1897*, II: 1092–93; Houston to Congress, November 21, 1837 in Amelia W. Williams and Eugene C. Barker, eds., *The Writings of Sam Houston*, II: 154; Houston *Telegraph and Texas Register*, November 23, 1837.

first it appeared that his hopes would be realized. After receiving favorable support from several sources, he concluded a contract on February 14, 1841, with Jacques Lafitte and Company of Paris for the loan. Hamilton was ecstatic. He notified the Texas government of his success, which awaited only the agreement of the French government to guarantee the loan. He estimated that barring unforeseen circumstances the entire operation would take about a month and the actual money would be in New York by July. With the loan seemingly assured, Hamilton appointed Henri Castro, an associate of the Lafitte Company, to handle the sale of Republic of Texas public lands that were designed to serve as security for the bonds. Unfortunately, the French Minister of Finance reported unfavorably on the project, which forced Hamilton to cancel the Lafitte contract.[4]

Meanwhile, Hamilton began negotiations with several other European countries. He traveled to the Netherlands, the German states, England, and Belgium. The greatest encouragement appeared to come from the Belgian representatives. Hamilton became convinced that the loan could be secured there. It seemed to require only a little negotiation before the deal would be consummated.[5]

The Republic of Texas faced a major credit problem because it used its public lands and the integrity of the new nation for collateral. Yet, the value of the public lands remained limited because the republic seemed unable to protect itself, and the integrity of a new and untried nation was not particularly attractive collateral. Beyond all this, however, the miserable failure of Texas to establish a stable financial situation

[4] William M. Gouge, *The Fiscal History of Texas*, 140; Houston *Telegraph and Texas Register*, January 16, 1841; Hamilton to Lipscomb, March 3, 1841, Hamilton to Castro February 11, 1841, in George P. Garrison, ed., *Diplomatic Correspondence of the Republic of Texas*, II: 1302, 1288; Houston *Telegraph and Texas Register*, June 30, July 7, and July 28, 1841; Hamilton to Secretary of State, November 3, 1841, in Seymour V. Connor, ed., *Texas Treasury Papers*, II: 1257.

[5] Hamilton to Lamar, May 17, 1841, Hamilton to Secretary of State, November 3, 1841, in Garrison, *Correspondence*, II: 1336–37, 1527–28. Although by law the loan was for $5 million, it was referred to by European countries in several forms. For example France usually termed it a $7 million loan, while in Belgium it was mentioned variously as being either for $4, $5, or $6 million. For consistency I will refer to it as the $5 million loan.

came as no particular surprise to an international community that faced similar difficulties.

Indeed, the leaders of the new nation viewed printing money and bond issues as only stopgap measures. They pinned their hope of establishing a sound financial basis on the sale of public lands. As early as 1837 Sam Houston spoke of the "boundless revenue" that would result from the opening of the General Land Office.[6] In mid-1842 he still held firm to that belief when he told Congress that "our vacant lands can be applied to the liquidation of every farthing of our national liabilities and a large portion still remain untouched."[7] After all, Texas had the example of the United States, which in 1836 actually had a surplus in the national treasury primarily because of the sale of its public domain. The solution seemed obvious. Attract a large population, sell that population the public lands, and the new nation would be solvent if not wealthy. Even if the public lands had to be given away, the increased population would create enough wealth for the country to be financially secure.[8]

To whet the appetite of expected immigrants Congress passed several land laws. It offered military bonuses in the form of land grants. Soldiers who served the Republic three months received 320 acres; six months, 640 acres; nine months, 960 acres; one year or more, 1,280 acres. The legislators patriotically granted land to the heirs of those killed at Goliad and the Alamo and to veterans of San Jacinto. Finally, they established the headright system as the major inducement to immigration. Congress, in 1836, voted the First Class Headright that guaranteed a league and a labor (4605.5 acres) of land free to anyone who settled in Texas prior to March 2, 1836, and had not received a Mexican grant. The First Class Headright was later extended to settlers before October 1, 1836, while the Second Class Headright was es-

[6] Houston to Congress, November 21, 1837, in Williams and Barker, *Writings*, II: 154; Houston *Telegraph and Texas Register*, November 23, 1837.

[7] Houston to Congress, June 27, 1842, in Williams and Barker, *Writings*, III: 81; Houston *Telegraph and Texas Register*, June 29, 1842.

[8] Anson Jones to Ashbel Smith, March 9, 1842, in Garrison, *Correspondence*, II: 949.

tablished to give each family head 1,280 acres and each single man 640 acres if they settled in Texas between October 1, 1836, and October 1, 1837. The expected immigration did not materialize, so in 1837 Congress established the Third Class Headright, which granted 640 acres to family heads and 320 acres to single men. Although twice extended, this attempt also proved unsuccessful and was terminated on January 1, 1840.[9]

As a result of this first attempt by the Republic of Texas to establish a general land policy and to attract a large population, land speculation became the largest single business activity in the nation. The headright and bonus grants were for a particular number of acres in any unclaimed area of the public domain. To obtain title to the acreage, the land first had to be located and surveyed, and then the survey notes had to be sent to the General Land Office. Land speculators bought the unlocated certificates in large numbers for low prices, expecting to sell them on a rising land market. When the price rise did not materialize, the certificates were traded either for specie or goods. Ultimately the practice of trading in land certificates became such a common occurrence that they almost assumed the character of legitimate currency.[10]

By 1840 it had become obvious to the leaders of the bankrupt nation that some sort of order had to be brought to the chaotic land situation. Among them there existed a preference for some type of empresario system similar to the one that had attracted the large United States emigration to Texas under the Mexican government. They felt that a much more orderly settlement of the country could be accomplished if responsible agents were given colonization contracts, which would shift the burden of attracting settlers from public to private means.

The first attempt at gaining an empresario contract from the Republic of Texas originated in the fertile imagination of

[9]Gammel, *Laws*, I: 1094, 1450; Thomas Lloyd Miller, *The Public Lands of Texas*, 27–57, contains a detailed discussion of the land-distribution policy of the Republic of Texas.

[10]Elgin Williams, *The Animating Pursuits of Speculation*, 91–95; Seymour V. Connor, "Land Speculation in Texas," *Southwest Review*, Spring, 1954, 138–43.

the newly appointed French chargé d'affaires, Dubois de Saligny. As early as 1839 he had estimated the population of Texas at 250,000 to 300,000 and projected a population of at least one million in less than five years. Although this was a wildly exaggerated figure concerning a region containing approximately 60,000 citizens, it was hyperbole typical of many impressionable European visitors.[11] Later he wrote that ". . . the Texian Government possesses 159,000,000 acres of land, the greater part of which is of the highest value. It can be readily sold and will bring a minimum of fifty cents per acre."[12] Obviously Saligny viewed the country as an area of tremendous opportunity that was not being exploited to its fullest possibilities.

Almost immediately on assuming his diplomatic post the Frenchman devised a plan to establish a French commercial monopoly in Texas. He had no problem interesting French business interests and brought to the attention of his government the benefit that could be gained from such an important outlet for French goods. Gaining influential Texas support was not so easily accomplished, but the wily little Frenchman wasted no time in seeking aid. Sam Houston and several other prominent Texans eventually supported his plan, which by the fall of 1840 was ready to become a reality.[13]

The plan appeared before the Texas Fifth Congress as the Franco-Texienne Bill. Devised by Saligny and two French businessmen, Jean Basterreche and Pierre Lassaulx, it was introduced into the House of Representatives by Congressman James Mayfield in mid-January. The bill proposed the establishment of a French company that would build a series of twenty forts, manned by French colonists, along the line of the western frontier from the Rio Grande to the Red River. In return for this service the company would receive three million acres of land on which it would locate 8,000 French

[11] Saligny to Mole, March 16, 1839, in Nancy Nichols Barker, ed., *The French Legation in Texas*, I: 69; *Senate Journal of the Republic of Texas, Sixth Congress*, I: 291–92; Elliott to Jones, August 17, 1843, in Jones, *Memoranda*, 247.

[12] Saligny to Dalmatia, June 24, 1839, in Barker, *Legation*, I: 101.

[13] Saligny to Dalmatia, May 4, 1840, in Barker, *Legation*, I: 141; John Henry Brown, *History of Texas*, II: 188.

settlers before January of 1849. As an inducement for the colonists to immigrate they would get free imports for twenty years and the company would not have to pay property taxes until after 1848. Additionally, the company would receive exclusive trading privileges with the towns of upper Mexico, rights to all mines found in the grant area, and no other companies or individuals would be granted land in the French concession area for a period of twenty years.[14]

Saligny felt sure there would be considerable Texas opposition to the proposal. Therefore he urged the French government to support Hamilton's efforts to secure the $5 million loan. This would create tremendous goodwill in Texas, and France would undoubtedly profit from the entire enterprise. Saligny even implied to the Texans that the loan was contingent on passage of the bill. At first glance this scheme seemed to be an excellent solution to the major problems faced by Texas. The line of forts manned by immigrant forces guaranteed protection against both Mexican armies and possible Indian raids. This protection would cost the republic nothing and the additional bait of the loan seemed to assure instant national solvency.[15]

Opposition to the bill soon developed, despite the seeming advantages. Political opponents of Sam Houston, led by President Lamar, launched a strong attack. The charges were many and varied, but opposition thinking centered on the fear that introduction of French military personnel coupled with massive French immigration to Texas would make the republic virtually a French colony. This had a telling effect on the Texas citizenry whose recent successful revolt against Mexico was fresh in their memories.[16]

Nevertheless, Houston's tremendous influence effected passage of the bill. It cleared the House on January 1, 1841,

[14] Saligny to Guizot, February 6, 1841, in Barker, *Legation*, I: 197; Austin *Texas Sentinel*, July 1, 1841; *Appendix to the Journals of the House of Representatives of the Republic of Texas, Fifth Congress*, 395–99; William C. Binkley, *The Expansionist Movement in Texas*, 54–56.

[15] Saligny to Dalmatia, May 4, 1840, in Barker, *Legation*, I: 141; Brown, *History of Texas*, II: 188; Binkley, *Expansionist Movement*, 55.

[16] Houston *Telegraph and Texas Register*, February 10, July 7, 1841; Austin *Texas Sentinel*, October 7, 1841.

by a vote of twenty to twelve, but received heavier opposition in the Senate where the Lamar faction had more strength. After amending the bill several times, the Senate deadlocked by a six-to-six vote after the second reading. Anson Jones, president pro tem of the Senate, broke the tie by voting in favor of the bill. Passage seemed assured. Then word came from the presidential office that the bill would be vetoed. Fearing that President Lamar's veto would kill action on the measure for all time, supporters of the Franco-Texienne Bill tabled the proposition with the expectation that it would be revived during the next congressional term.[17]

In the midst of the heated debate over the Franco-Texienne Bill, Congress passed the single most momentous piece of legislation affecting Republic of Texas empresario concessions. In a memorial presented to Congress sometime before January 14, 1841, a group of men headed by W. S. Peters requested an empresario concession. This request resulted in the passage, on February 4, 1841, of A Law Granting Land to Immigrants. This law became the basis for all empresario grants made under the auspices of the Republic of Texas. It consisted of two basic divisions. The first section dealt with continuing the headright system, while the second established the ground rules whereby the Peters group would receive an empresario contract. The first section of the law of February 4, 1841, continued the headright system, which still had not attracted the expected large population. It extended the Third Class Headright to January 1, 1842, and made it retroactive to January 1, 1840. Every head of a household received 640 acres and every single man 320 acres. For them to qualify for the land they had to live on it for three years, cultivate a minimum of ten acres, have the property surveyed, and register with the chief justice of the county when the terms were legally fulfilled.

<hr/>

[17] *Journal of the House of Representatives of the Republic of Texas, Fifth Congress, First Session*, 597; *Senate Journal of the Republic of Texas, Fifth Congress, First Session*, 187; Austin *Texas Sentinel*, July 1, 1841; Saligny to Guizot, February 6, 1841, in Barker, *Legation*, I: 197. For a detailed account of the Franco-Texienne Bill see Bernice Barrett Denton, "Count Alphonso de Saligny and the Franco-Texienne Bill," *Southwestern Historical Quarterly* 45 (October, 1941): 136–46.

The second section of the bill empowered the president of the republic to enter into an empresario contract with the twenty petitioners headed by W. S. Peters. The terms of the contract called for one-third of the number of colonists specified in the contract to be settled within one year, although the president could grant a six-month extension at his discretion. However, the full terms of the contract had to be met within three years. Colonists who were heads of households received 640 acres and single men over seventeen years of age received 320 acres. The empresarios received ten sections of bonus land from the republic for every one hundred heads of households and five sections of land for every one hundred single men settled on the grant. In addition the empresario could charge the colonist a fee for expenses of up to one-half the land each settler was to receive.[18]

Not until August 8, 1841, did the Peters group sign a contract with President Lamar. Eventually the republic made three additional contracts with the Peters group. The limits of the total grant were extensive. The land began at a point on the Red River and ran a hundred miles south, passing just east of Dallas. From there it ran west for 164 miles before turning north to the Red River and then followed the river to the point of origin. The eastern edge of the grant included the counties of Dallas, Collin, and Grayson, while the western boundary included Wilbarger, Baylor, Throckmorton, and Shackelford counties. This tremendous grant of land was designed to protect the north and northwest borders of the republic.[19]

When the Fifth Congress adjourned without passing the Franco-Texienne Bill, an infuriated Saligny retired to New Orleans to sulk and plan some other means by which he might regain an advantage. Both Basterreche and Lassaulx, who had been in Texas lobbying for the bill, returned to France. Nevertheless, Saligny still entertained some hope of getting the bill reintroduced in the Sixth Congress. Most of his opti-

---

[18] *Journal of the House*, 508; Gammel, *Laws*, II: 554–56, 663.

[19] Seymour V. Connor, *The Peters Colony of Texas* contains the most detailed discussion available of the Peters Colony, the extent of its holdings, and its importance to Texas.

mism was based on the expectation that Sam Houston would gain the presidency in the 1841 elections. His hopes soared when Houston was elected, and the bill was once again ready to be introduced into Congress.[20]

Meanwhile, several Europeans with concerns about the Texas financial situation converged on the republic. One of them, Capt. Victor Pirson, was a member of a prominent Belgian family. As recently as 1840 he had been attached to the Belgian legation at Constantinople, but on October 7, 1841, he became secretary to the legation at New York charged with a special mission to Texas. His assignment was to tour the republic and investigate its finances, resources, and relations with other nations to determine if the Belgian government should guarantee the $5 million loan Hamilton was trying to negotiate.[21]

Hamilton met Pirson in London for the first leg of the trip and promised that Belgium would receive the contested territory between the Rio Grande and the Nueces for colonization in the event the loan was successful. The Belgian was supposed to travel to Texas with the general, but Hamilton had other pressing affairs to conduct and arranged to meet Pirson in New Orleans as soon as possible. Pirson then proceeded on to the United States, reported to his post in New York, and stopped by the Belgian embassy in Washington, D.C., before going on to New Orleans.[22]

While in Washington during December of 1841 Pirson met Henri Castro who was also on his way to Texas. Castro was traveling as the personal envoy of Jacques Lafitte with the assigned task of checking on the feasibility of getting the $5 million loan consummated. Basterreche and Lassaulx also

[20] Saligny to Guizot, January 6, 1842, in Barker, *Legation*, I: 275.

[21] Mary Katherine Chase, *Négociations de la Republique du Texas en Europe*, fn. 91–92; de Briey to Pirson, November 13, 1841, Archives of the Belgium Foreign Office, Mission Pirson, as cited in Chase, *Négociations*, 92; Kennedy to Earl of Aberdeen, April 20, 1842, in Ephraim Douglass Adams, ed., *British Diplomatic Correspondence Concerning the Republic of Texas*, 62; Hamilton to Jones, February 18, 1842, Hamilton to Secretary of State, November 3, 1841, in Garrison, *Correspondence*, II: 946, 1528.

[22] Pirson to de Briey, November 18, 1841, Archives of the Belgium Foreign Office, Mission Pirson, as cited in Chase, *Négociations*, 94.

had empowered him to act in their behalf in trying to get the Franco-Texienne Bill passed by the Sixth Texas Congress. Thus the Belgian and the Frenchman, both on missions of a similar nature, traveled the 1,019 miles from Washington to New Orleans together. This journey provided ample time for them to discuss fully opportunities for land acquisition in Texas.[23]

Henri Castro in 1842 was a fifty-five-year-old citizen of France with a varied background in finance. He was from a Jewish family that had emigrated from Portugal to France sometime prior to Henri's birth in 1786. As a young man Castro had held several minor political positions in his native Department of Landes and even served in the Napoleonic army. Afterward he lived for a time in the United States, where he acted as the consul for Naples at the Port of Providence, Rhode Island. During that period he became involved in East Coast banking activity and learned to speak excellent English. By 1838 he had returned to Paris, where he became associated with the Lafitte banking interests and through that work met Gen. James Hamilton. Eventually those connections led to his return to the United States to investigate investment possibilities in Texas.[24]

Castro and Pirson arrived in New Orleans on January 15, 1842, and on the following day both of them met with Saligny. The chargé d'affaires made certain of Pirson's business, and then visited at length with Castro. Saligny, when fully satisfied with Castro's intention to get the Franco-Texienne Bill passed, gave him a letter of introduction to Anson Jones, Texas Secretary of State. Saligny emphasized in the letter

[23] Pirson to de Briey, January 15, 1842, Archives of the Belgium Foreign Office, Mission Pirson, as cited in Chase, *Négociations*, 97; Saligny to Guizot, January 16, 1842, in Barker, *Legation*, I: 278.

[24] Henry Cohen, "Henry Castro: Pioneer and Colonist," *Publications of the American Jewish Historical Society*, no. 5, 1896, 1–5; Henry Cohen, "Early Jewish Settlements in Texas," in *One Hundred Years of Jewry in Texas*, 13–15; August Fretelliere, "Adventures d'un Castrovillain," August Fretelliere Papers, Barker Texas History Center, University of Texas at Austin, 1–2; Henri Castro, "Le Texas," Henri Castro Papers, Barker Texas History Center, University of Texas at Austin, 1–3; Samuel Swartwout to Sam Houston, December 26, 1841, in Feris A. Bass, Jr., and B. R. Brunson, eds., *Fragile Empires: The Texas Correspondence of Samuel Swartwout and James Morgan, 1836–1856*, 154–57.

that the bearer had full powers to negotiate for Basterreche and Lassaulx. But he further stated that if Congress rejected the bill, Castro would appreciate any help he could get in other matters.[25]

Castro left New Orleans immediately and reached Austin by January 29. The letter of recommendation, which also allowed him to use the French-legation building as a headquarters, made him a welcome visitor in Austin. President Houston particularly enjoyed the lavish hospitality afforded by the Frenchman at the legation. Unfortunately, the congressional session was too far advanced to permit debate and adoption of the Franco-Texienne Bill. Nevertheless, Castro continued to entertain Texas political leaders in the hope that something could be salvaged from the wreck of the plan that he had been sent to consummate.[26]

Word of the activities of the French and Belgian agents in Texas did not escape the attention of the British government. Although unwilling to take official action, Lord Aberdeen, British Minister of Foreign Affairs, appointed William Kennedy an unofficial agent to go to Texas and keep an eye on developments. Kennedy was a particularly good choice because he had spent most of 1839 in the republic, and in 1841 had published a book-length account of his observations concerning the new country. His book, which was very favorable in its description of Texas, won him many influential friends in the new nation.[27]

The British agent received his appointment on November 9, 1841, left England on November 19, and arrived at Galveston on January 9, 1842. Coincidentally, Kennedy left England on the same day as Pirson, the Belgian agent, but evidently he did not tarry along the way because he was in Galveston a full week before Pirson and Castro arrived in

---

[25] Saligny to Guizot, January 16, 1842, in Barker, *Legation* I: 278–80; Saligny to Jones, January 16, 1842, in Garrison, *Correspondence*, II: 1353–54.

[26] Saligny to Guizot, February 17, 1842, Saligny to Guizot, February 26, 1842, in Barker, *Legation*, I: 287, 290.

[27] Kennedy to Aberdeen, October 10, October 20, November 6, and November 9, 1841, in Adams, *British Correspondence*, 43, 45, 46, and 48; Saligny to Guizot, February 17, 1842, in Barker, *Legation*, I: 288; Harriet Smither, *Journals of the Sixth Congress of the Republic of Texas*, II: 70, 139–40, 408.

New Orleans. By the time the Frenchman got to Austin, Kennedy had firmly situated himself in the capital and had become a man well worth having as an ally.[28]

As the various European agents began to gather in Texas in their official, semi-official, and unofficial capacities, the Texas Congress began wrestling with the problem of public-land distribution. The Franco-Texienne Bill was out of the question since it had fallen into general public disfavor. Consequently, Congress passed a bill for general land distribution, which Houston promptly vetoed. The bill, hastily rewritten as an amendment to the "Peters Colony" Bill, became law on February 5, 1842. It simply empowered the president to make empresario contracts with persons he deemed fit under the same stipulations enunciated in the Peters Colony Bill. Thus the president received authority to accomplish what he had wanted under the Franco-Texienne Bill—that is, to protect the southern and western borders, without making unpopular commercial concessions.[29]

Application for land concessions came quickly. Castro and Kennedy joined forces. On February 3 Castro became Consul General of Texas to France, while Kennedy became Consul General of Texas to Great Britain. On February 5, the day the new colonization law was passed, Castro and Kennedy jointly asked for a grant of land in the general vicinity of the unsuccessful Beals Colony attempt under the Mexican government. Kennedy, who was familiar with that region, had previously described it as an excellent area for settlement.[30]

Actually Castro and Kennedy requested two separate tracts of land. They were

1. A tract commencing at a point where the Upper Presidio del Rio Road crosses the River Nueces and extending to the headwaters

[28]Kennedy to Aberdeen, January 10, 1842, in Adams, *British Correspondence*, 51.

[29]Houston to House of Representatives, June 31, 1842, in Williams and Barker, *Writings*, II: 456–57; Gammel, *Laws*, II: 785–86.

[30]Kennedy to Aberdeen, March 25, 1842, in Adams, *British Correspondence*, 59–60; Houston to Texas Senate, February 3, 1842, Houston to Kennedy and Castro, February 5, 1842, in Williams and Barker, *Writings*, II: 472 and III: 73; William Kennedy, *Texas: The Rise, Progress, and Prospects of the Republic of Texas*, 168–71.

of the river Leona; thence to the dividing ridge between the waters of the rivers Medina and Frio, twenty miles north of the upper Presidio Road; thence along said dividing ridge to the Laredo Road. . . . Thence along the road to the point where it crosses the river Nueces . . . and thence up the stream of the Nueces to the crossing of the Upper Presidio Road.

2. A tract twenty miles in breadth commencing at a point on the Rio Grande ten miles above Dolores Ferry, and stretching downwards along the left bank to the road from the Salt Lakes to Camargo on the said river.[31]

When the government issued the contracts on February 15, 1842, it divided the originally requested land with Kennedy and Castro receiving separate grants. Castro's grant, in partnership with Jean Jassaud, another Lafitte and Company associate,[32] consisted of two tracts described as

Tract number one commencing at the Laredo crossing on the left bank of the Rio Frio, thence along the Laredo Road to the dividing ridge of the Rio Frio and the Medina waters, to a point equidistant from the two rivers, thence with that range as nearly equidistant as practical as above, to a point twenty miles above the Upper Presidio del Rio Grande Road, thence in a direct line to the point of the confluence of the Arroyo de Uvalde with the Rio Frio, thence down the main branch of the Rio Frio to the point of commencement.

Tract number two lay in the land bordering the Rio Grande that Castro and Kennedy originally requested. The president divided the original Rio Grande request into four equal parts, numbered one through four from the lower portion of the area to the upper portion. Castro and Jassaud received the number one part or the section farthest down the river and grant number three.[33]

Kennedy received his grant with William Pringle, Ken-

---

[31] As cited in Audrey Goldthorp, "Castro's Colony" (Master's thesis, University of Texas, 1935), 63.

[32] Jacques Lafitte, "Le Emprunt," Henri Castro Papers, 234.

[33] The only complete text of the contract can be found in the Austin *Texas State Gazette*, October 27, 1849. Summaries or portions of the contract are located in the Colonization Papers, Archives, Texas State Library, Austin; Williams and Barker, *Writings*, II: 483–84; and the Houston *Telegraph and Texas Register*, July 13, 1842.

nedy's London lawyer. Their main grant included the portion of the original request described as

Commencing at a point where the Upper Presidio del Rio Grande Road crosses the river Nueces, and extending thence in a direct line to the head spring of the river Leona, including the said spring, then in a direct line to the point of confluence of the Arroyo de Uvalde with the Rio Frio, thence down the main branch of the Rio Frio to the crossing of the road from San Antonio to Laredo, thence along the line of said road to the river Nueces, thence along the east bank of the said River to the point of beginning.

The Englishmen's portion of the Rio Grande land consisted of tracts two and four of the original request.[34]

Several other Europeans also took advantage of the colonization law as soon as it became operative. Henry F. Fisher and Burchard Miller requested a grant on February 8, 1842, but they did not follow through and get their contract signed until June 7, 1842. The Fisher-Miller grant was unusual because it was rechartered on September 1, 1843. This grant was the largest 1842 contract signed. Because of inaccurate geographical information, an error on the western boundary of the Fisher-Miller grant made it impossible to ascertain the exact western limits, but the grant did contain approximately nine million acres.[35]

While these activities were taking place Pirson, the Belgian agent, arrived in Austin. There he found himself without a basis for his original mission, because on January 26 the government cancelled Hamilton's authority to negotiate the $5 million loan. Nevertheless, Pirson remained in Texas, traveled extensively, and became well acquainted with Houston and various other government officials. Because of this activity, on February 26 Anson Jones offered him a colonization contract, which the Belgian accepted on March 9, after a

[34] Colonization Papers; William Bollaert, *William Bollaert's Texas*, 380–84.

[35] Colonization Papers; Williams and Barker, *Writings*, III: 428; Report of the Department of State to the Texas Senate, Houston *Telegraph and Texas Register*, July 13, 1842; Solon Ollie Loving, "A History of the Fisher-Miller Land Grant from 1842–1860" (Master's thesis, University of Texas, 1934), 26; Moritz Tiling, *History of the German Element in Texas from 1820–1850*, 69.

long conference with Houston in which they agreed the contract would be official only if it was approved by the Belgian
government.[36]

The Pirson grant consisted of two parcels of land located
on the Rio Grande. The first joined the Castro-Jassaud grant
or block number one and extended out from the river twenty-
five miles and down the river fifty miles. The second concession joined the Kennedy-Pringle upper grant or block number four and extended out from the river twenty-five miles
and up the river fifty miles. Nothing came of the effort because the Belgian government never sanctioned the concession as a result of a conflict with a colonization project already underway in Guatemala.[37]

The increasing activity in Texas prompted the French
Minister of Commerce to send a semi-official agent to the republic to study and report on the economic situation there.
The man selected for the job was Alexandre Bourgeois
d'Orvanne, a former mayor of Clichy-la-Garenne and prominent businessman. Bourgeois took advantage of the appointment to have the first French merchant ship sent to Texas.
He arrived later on the *Atlante* in early February, 1842,
along with eighty other French immigrants. One of these
passengers was Armand Ducos, former subprefect of Civray.
Ducos came to Texas to seek the title for a land concession from the Mexican government to a French citizen. Meeting on the trip over, the two Frenchmen formed a close
relationship.[38]

Ducos failed in his bid to salvage the grant for which he
had been sent. But Bourgeois traveled extensively, took volu-
minous notes, and generally went about the business of com-

[36] Hamilton to Jones, February 18, 1842, in Garrison, *Correspondence*, 947;
Jones, *Memoranda*, 38; Pirson to de Briey, February 8, 1842, and March 10, 1842,
Archives of the Belgium Foreign Office, Mission Pirson, as cited in Chase, *Négocia-
tions*, 102, 103.

[37] Jones to Pirson, March 9, 1842, Goblet to Pirson, May 13, 1843, Archives
of the Belgium Foreign Office, Mission Pirson, as cited in Chase, *Négociations*,
204–205, 116; Jones to Smith, December 26, 1842, in Garrison, *Correspondence*, II:
1409.

[38] Saligny to Guizot, February 17, June 11, 1842, in Barker, *Legation* I: 287,
336.

pleting his task. It did not take Bourgeois and Ducos long to decide that a colonization contract could be very profitable. Accordingly, they approached Saligny about the advisability of such a scheme. With the aid of the French chargé d'affaires the two Frenchmen on June 3, 1842, received two concessions that totaled 3 million acres.[39] Their main grant joined Castro's on the north and the west:

Beginning at the junction of the Potranco and the Rio Medina: thence up the Potranco to its source; thence due north to the Sabinas, thence in a direct line to the source of the Arroyo de Uvalde; thence in a direct line to the source of the southern branch of the Rio Frio; thence extending down said stream to the junction of the Rio Frio and the Arroyo de Uvalde; thence along the line of the grant made to Henri Castro and Jean Jassaud to the northeast corner of said grant; thence in a direct line to the place of beginning.

They also received a Rio Grande Concession that extended from the mouth of the river to the town of Reinosa and out from the river for ten miles.[40]

In addition to influencing the land concession, Saligny arranged for Bourgeois to get a contract to negotiate a $1 million loan in France for the republic. The terms specified that the Cherokee lands in East Texas would be reserved for use as compensation if Bourgeois succeeded in negotiating the loan. With the land concession in hand and a signed contract assuring him of extensive East Texas acreage if he could consummate the loan, Bourgeois left for France on June 14 filled with unbounded optimism.[41]

Indeed, all the empresarios of 1842 had reason to anticipate a bright future. The unfavorable press that had bitterly opposed the Franco-Texienne Bill generally favored the new land concessions. According to the Houston *Telegraph and*

[39]Saligny to Guizot, June 8, 1842, in Barker, *Legation*, I: 336–37; Bollaert, *Texas*, 100, 102.

[40]Report of the Department of State to the Texas Senate, Houston *Telegraph and Texas Register*, July 13, 1842.

[41]Saligny to Guizot, June 8, 1842, in Barker, *Legation*, I: 337; Houston to Jones, June 10, 1842, in Williams and Barker, *Writings*, II: 66; Jones, *Memoranda*, 25, 203; Smith to Jones, August 1, 1842, Jones to Smith, December 23, 1842, in Garrison, *Correspondence*, II: 1382, 1406.

REPUBLIC of TEXAS EMPRESARIO LAND GRANTS:

1841 - 1842

Texas Register individual grants like those given to Bourgeois and Ducos presented little if any reason for conflict between Texas and the European powers. Indeed, its editorial writer thought that the business acumen of the new empresarios would assure both them and Texas a secure future.[42]

The basic terms of the five concessions granted in 1842 remained the same as those stated in the Peters Colony law of February 4, 1841. Each empresario had three years to complete his contract, but he must have one-third of the contracted numbers of colonists in Texas within one year, subject to a six-month extension by the president. The contractor would be compensated with ten sections of land for every one hundred heads of households he introduced or with five sections for every one hundred single men over the age of seventeen. The contractor could charge his colonists a fee not to exceed one-half of their alloted land in payment for expenses incurred. A colonist must build a cabin, cultivate fifteen acres of land, and live on the property for three years in order to gain title to the property.[43]

The location of the various grants approximated the territory desired by the Franco-Texienne Land Company. The numbers of colonists varied considerably, however, from grant to grant. The Fisher-Miller concession called for 600 families with the privilege of increasing the number to 6,000. Castro and Jassaud received a basic contract for 600 families that could be increased to 1,000. Bourgeois and Ducos acquired two separate groups. On the main grant they contracted to settle 1,200 families with the privilege of increasing to 1,600, while on their Rio Grande concession they had the right to introduce an additional 500 families. The Kennedy-Pringle Concession required the same number as Castro's, 600 with the privilege of increasing to 1,000. This same number, 600 to 1,000, was also allowed Pirson along the Rio Grande.[44] If all the contracts were completed, the re-

[42] Houston *Telegraph and Texas Register*, June 8, 1842.
[43] Gammel, *Laws*, II: 554–56, 663.
[44] Houston *Telegraph and Texas Register*, July 13, 1842; Jones to Pirson, Archives of the Belgium Foreign Office, Mission Pirson, as cited in Chase, *Négociations*, 204–205.

public could expect a minimum increase of 4,100 to 10,600 landholders, or a population increase of 12,000 to 30,000 people. This arrangement showed considerable advantage over the 8,000 colonists called for in the Franco-Texienne Bill, and as an added bonus, it had no entangling financial arrangements.

Thus by late 1842 Texans appeared to have solved part of their basic problem of finance and population. The specter of financial collapse forced the Texas government to resort to an empresario system to ease its difficulties. That decision distributed land grants among several individuals representing populations in various parts of western Europe. The lucky empresarios felt they had the opportunity of a lifetime: a fortune seemed to lie within their grasp. Throughout 1842 the recipients of the grants left Texas and returned to their respective countries to set up the apparatus to recruit settlers for Texas public lands. As activities escalated, it is doubtful that either the Texans or the empresarios fully understood the implications of the series of events they were about to set in motion.

CHAPTER II

The Project Begins

OBTAINING their contracts was only the first step, and perhaps the easiest part, of the work facing the empresarios of 1842. Castro and his fellow contractors with the Republic of Texas had to implement a recruiting program in Europe capable of placing a specific number of colonists on the grants within two years. If they were to succeed in this work, there was no time to be lost.

The sense of well-being engendered in Castro and Kennedy by receiving empresario contracts did not obscure the urgent need to implement a colonization program. Both men departed Austin a few days after getting their contracts approved. The Englishman left immediately for Europe, but Castro remained at Galveston awaiting Ashbel Smith, the newly appointed Texas ambassador to France. Castro and Smith left Texas in mid-March and traveled to New Orleans, where the Frenchman assisted in making several beneficial financial arrangements for the republic. Because of this delay it was mid-May before the empresario reached France and began his recruiting program.[1]

[1] William Kennedy to Ashbel Smith, March 12, 1842, in Ernest W. Winkler, ed., *Manuscript Letters and Documents of Early Texians*, 253; William Kennedy to Lord Aberdeen, April 20, 1842, in Ephraim Douglass Adams, ed., *British Diplomatic Correspondence Concerning the Republic of Texas*, 61; Kennedy sold his concession to a group of British investors who never developed it. For a fuller description of the Kennedy concession and its ultimate disposition consult William Bollaert, *William Bollaert's Texas*, W. Eugene Hollan and Ruth Lapham Butler, eds; Ashbel Smith to Anson Jones, March 16, 1842, Ashbel Smith to McIntosh, May 23, 1842, in George P. Garrison, ed., *Diplomatic Correspondence of the Republic of Texas*, II: 1359–61, 1374; Saligny to Guizot, March 16, 1842, in Nancy Nichols Barker, ed., *The French Legation in Texas*, I: 293.

This kind of work suited Henri Castro very well. At the age of fifty-five when many men were settled in some secure position he had promoted his empresario contract. He impressed associates as an unusually articulate and persuasive negotiator who dressed stylishly and enjoyed an almost lavish life-style. They described him in this period of his life as being of medium height, well dressed, and possessing a forthright demeanor that inspired confidence. This mature individual, with his excellent command of English and impressive background in finance, appeared well qualified to pursue the colonization project.[2]

Castro's capacity for influencing people soon faced a severe test. By the time he reached Paris news had preceded him of the March invasion of Texas by a hostile Mexican force that actually captured San Antonio before retiring across the Rio Grande. This news had a decidedly adverse effect upon his recruiting of potential settlers. Few wanted to leave Europe for a frontier region that was open to aggression by a hostile military force at any time.[3]

Meanwhile, political problems surfaced when Castro presented his appointment as Texas consul general to France for approval by the French foreign ministry. Objections to the empresario's appointment originated in New Orleans with Dubois de Saligny, the French chargé d'affaires to Texas. When he heard that Castro was unsuccessful in promoting the Franco-Texienne Bill in which Saligny had an interest but had gotten a land concession for himself instead, Saligny turned against Castro. The chargé began to send unfavorable reports to the French home office concerning Castro's

<hr />

[2] Henry Cohen, "Henry Castro: Pioneer and Colonist," *Publications of the American Jewish Historical Society*, no. 5, 1896, 1–5; Henry Cohen, "Early Jewish Settlements in Texas," in *One Hundred Years of Jewry in Texas*, 13–15; August Fretelliere, "Adventures d'un Castrovillain," August Fretelliere Papers, Barker Texas History Center, University of Texas at Austin, 1–2; Henri Castro, "Le Texas," Henri Castro Papers, Barker Texas History Center, The University of Texas at Austin; Samuel Swartwout to Sam Houston, December 26, 1841, in Feris A. Bass, Jr., and B. R. Brunson, eds., *Fragile Empire: The Texas Correspondence of Samuel Swartwout and James Morgan, 1836–1856*, 154–57.

[3] Anson Jones to Castro, January 4, 1843, Colonization Papers, Archives, Texas State Library, Austin.

character. He spread rumors that Castro was a Portuguese Jew, a scoundrel, and that he was living in "open fornication" with his wife's daughter in Paris. Further, he swore that Castro had been involved in fraudulent stock market and banking schemes in New York where he had stolen a considerable amount of money. These reports did considerable damage to Castro's reputation, particularly in France.[4]

The rumors concerning the empresario soon came to the attention of Sam Houston. Alarmed at the possibility of having made a mistake in trusting Castro, President Houston ordered Ashbel Smith, who was in Paris by this time, to observe carefully Castro's activities. Houston ordered Smith to withdraw Castro's appointment as consul general to France at the first sign of any untoward conduct. This action proved unnecessary when in August the French foreign minister, François Pierre Guizot, rejected Castro's application to become consul general. Thus Saligny successfully blocked any political advantage the empresario might have had in France.[5]

Regardless of any opposition to his plans or to him personally, Castro realized that he was working against a deadline. According to his contract he had to have at least 200 potential landholders in Texas before August 15, 1843, or forfeit his agreement. With this deadline spurring him on when he arrived in Paris in May, he took luxurious quarters at 18 Rue de Lafitte in Paris and began the work of recruiting French colonists. In that sumptuous setting Castro met potential colonists and overwhelmed them with an overpowering sense of his status and ability. Those who visited him there came away convinced that if they could only get to

[4]McIntosh to Ashbel Smith, May 18, 1842, Castro to Ashbel Smith, May 23, 1842, in Garrison, *Correspondence*, II: 1375–76; Saligny to Guizot, March 16, April 11, 1842, in Barker, *Legation*, I: 293, 300–303; Morgan to Swartwout, June 23, 1842, in Bass and Brunson, *Fragile Empires*, 183.

[5]Anson Jones to Ashbel Smith, June 7, 1842, in Garrison, *Correspondence*, II: 964; Ashbel Smith to Anson Jones, August 15, 1842, Texas Department of State Copybooks of Diplomatic Correspondence, 1836–42, Letters Received, Archives, Texas State Library, Austin, 139. Although Guizot informed Smith that Castro would not be accepted as consul general in August, the official statement did not appear until October. See Ashbel Smith to Anson Jones, October 31, 1842, in Garrison, *Correspondence*, II: 1391.

Texas it would be simply a matter of time until they could
turn a modest investment into millions.[6]

During the summer, after news of the unfortunate events
in Texas and during the controversy surrounding Castro's
appointment as consul general, the empresario continued
the work of implementing a colonization program. He organized the Société de Colonisation Europée–Américain au
Texas whose central agency was located at 6 rue de la Beaume
in Paris. Through this organization Castro hired agents to
recruit colonists and devised the means to insure the orderly
movement of emigrants from France to Texas.[7]

Castro developed a contractural arrangement whereby
potential colonists signed agreements to emigrate to the colony and Castro agreed to furnish the land. The contracts,
which remained fairly standard throughout the life of the
colonization program, paraphrased the law that granted Castro his concession and outlined the stipulations of his contract. Castro attached to the colonial contract an additional
statement, legal under the contract terms, which relinquished
to Castro one-half the land due to the colonist in return for
expenses incurred by the empresario in recruiting and transporting the colonist to the property. This meant that every
married man who was to get 640 acres promised to deed over
320 acres to Castro, and every single man who was to get 320
acres was to deed over 160 acres to Castro before they could
become legal colonists. After the colonist signed both the
contract and the land waiver, he was required to put up a deposit of 100 francs ($20), which he could redeem upon ar-
rival on concession land. This fee insured that the person
would indeed go to the colony or forfeit his deposit. This arrangement gave considerable protection to Castro against
losing any potential colonist as well as assuring a method

    [6]Austin *Texas State Gazette*, October 27, 1849; Ashbel Smith to Anson Jones,
December 30, 1842, in Garrison, *Correspondence*, II: 1066–67; Fretelliere, "Adventures," 1–2.
    [7]Société de Colonisation Europée-Américaine au Texas, "Avis au immigrants
sémbarquens au Havre," Ben R. Franklin File. James Menke Collection, San Antonio; Castro to Anson Jones, February 20, 1843. Colonization Papers.

of regaining any expense incurred during the recruitment process.[8]

Once the contract was signed and the deposit made, each emigrant received detailed written instructions on what to do, whom to see, and where to go in regard to the colonization project. These instructions included information about customs, train schedules to the port of embarkation, places to stay and the cost of lodging at the port, food and cooking utensils to take on the voyage, and finally, whom to contact and where to stay upon arrival at New Orleans and Galveston. Perhaps most important, at least to the colonization company, the society requested that each colonist keep a journal of his observations on the voyage so it could use the information to improve conditions for later colonists and also to prove to other potential recruits that the enterprise was worthwhile.[9]

One bright spot did appear during the early stages of the project when Ashbel Smith gave his approval to Castro's efforts. The Texas ambassador closely observed the empresario's work as instructed by the Texas government and was very impressed with the energetic activities that were taking place. He reported back to Texas that the empresario was indeed honest and sincere and that much of the bad publicity surrounding Castro resulted from jealousy and internal French political machinations. Nevertheless, problems continued to hinder the project. Castro became particularly upset by the concession granted Bourgeois and Ducos in June, 1842. Castro believed that he had the exclusive right to conduct emigration from France to Texas and vehemently protested that the Texas government had violated its agreement. He even went so far as to ask Ashbel Smith to issue state-

---

[8] Numerous examples of these contracts exist in various repositories including Blevins Papers, Witte Museum Library, San Antonio; Leinweber File, James Menke Collection, San Antonio; and Colonization Papers, Archives, Texas State Library, Austin. Perhaps the most detailed description of a Castro colonist contract appears in Audrey Goldthorp, "Castro's Colony" (Master's thesis, University of Texas, 1928), 68–69; Castro to Anson Jones, November 1, 1842, Colonization Papers.

[9] Société de Colonisation, "Avis au immigrants."

ments to the press stating that the Bourgeois concession was illegal. But Smith firmly informed him that Bourgeois had every right to recruit in France. Then in September Mexican forces again invaded Texas, captured San Antonio, and returned to Mexico with prisoners. When this news reached Europe it further hindered recruiting.[10]

Despite the bad news from Texas, competition from Bourgeois, and opposition from the French government, Castro managed to send his first colonial ship to Texas during 1842. On November 2 the *Ebro* left Le Havre bound for Galveston with 144 colonists aboard. This number included 42 persons eligible to receive land under contract stipulations. The *Lyons* followed on January 18, 1843, from Le Havre bound for New Orleans with 91 colonists, of whom 29 were eligible to receive land. On February 27 the *Louis Philippe* sailed from Dunquerque for Galveston with 49 passengers representing 23 eligible landholders. Also recruited were two bachelors eligible to receive land, who sailed independently of the regularly scheduled vessels. Thus, before the end of February, 1843, Castro embarked 96 potential landholders before suspending operations until autumn.[11]

Finding suitable colonists proved to be a difficult problem. At least half the 96 potential landholders sent on the first three ships listed occupations other than farmer. Castro had specific instructions from the Texas government to send only those who came prepared with munitions, clothing, and provisions to last them six months. When the *Ebro* left, Castro described in glowing terms those immigrants as well prepared with tools and money, classifying some of them as even wealthy. Yet the records of the first three vessels indicate that the empresario was not altogether truthful. Of the ninety-six

[10] Ashbel Smith to Anson Jones, October 31, November 2, November 13, December 30, 1842, and March 31, 1843, Castro to Ashbel Smith, May 23, 1842, Anson Jones to Ashbel Smith, December 26, 1842, Garrison, *Correspondence*, II: 1391; 1392, 1396, 1066–67, 1430, 1375–76, 1409; Anson Jones to Castro, January 4, 1843, Castro to Anson Jones, October 15, 1842, Colonization Papers.

[11] "List of Colonists sent to Texas by the ship *Ebro*," Castro to Anson Jones, April 1, 1843, "List of colonists sent to Texas by the ship Lyons," "List of Colonists sent to Texas by the ship Louis Phillippe," Colonization Papers; Ashbel Smith to Anson Jones, March 31, 1843, Garrison, *Correspondence*, II: 1430.

households represented, complete records remain for only seventy-nine, but of those eleven showed no property at all, while another seventeen had $100 or less. Only seventeen households indicated property of more than $500, while the balance fell somewhere between $100 and $300. In view of Castro's instructions to provide for his people, the Republic of Texas was not likely to welcome most of these immigrants, who would only aggravate an already critical financial situation.[12]

Castro was certain that his contract would be voided if he did not send the prescribed number of colonists to Texas before the initial time period of eighteen months lapsed. Furthermore, his situation seemed even more desperate because he had not made firm arrangements for an agent in Texas to receive the colonists and look after their interests. To give a semblance of leadership to the enterprise he appointed Albert Laude and François Phene, sailing on the *Ebro*, as directors of colonization in Texas. This evidently represented only a device to gain time and to give the scheme a sense of respectability, because the two bachelors, who were only nineteen and twenty-three years of age, respectively, never really assumed any leadership role in the operation. Apparently Castro realized this, for he named Elizie Martin of Lyon, on the *Louis Philippe*, director general of the colonists. Once again there is no evidence that Martin, a forty-two year old bachelor, ever assumed any leadership role. Indeed, he never received any colony land and probably returned to France after a short stay in Texas.[13]

Castro also faced the troublesome problem of commu-

[12] Sam Houston to William Henry Daingerfield, April 9, 1843, in Amelia W. Williams and Eugene C. Barker, eds., *The Writings of Sam Houston*, III: 20; Castro to Anson Jones, October 15, November 1, 1842, Colonization Papers; Castro to Anson Jones, November 15, 1842, Texas, Department of State Copybooks, 201–202; this information was compiled from an analysis of the property columns on the ships' lists of the *Ebro*, the *Lyons*, and the *Louis Philippe* in the Colonization Papers.

[13] Castro to Anson Jones, November 1, 1842, February 20, 1843, Colonization Papers; Sam Houston to Major George T. Howard, January 24, 1842, in Williams and Barker, *Writings*, II: 440; Castro to Anson Jones, November 12, 1842, Texas Department of State Copybooks, 195; Ship's List for the *Ebro*, Colonization Papers. Laude never again appears on the records, but Phene remained in Texas, received a land grant on concession property, and as late as 1855 was living in Houston.

nicating with Texas. From May through September of 1842 he sent at least one letter each month to Texas Secretary of State Anson Jones, keeping him informed of the progress of the colonization project. Jones received none of those dispatches except for one letter dated September 15, which arrived in Texas during mid-November. Naturally this long silence created an atmosphere of suspicion on both sides. Jones assumed that Castro was doing little or nothing, while Castro feared that Texas was not supporting him in his work.[14]

Beginning in October when the empresario was sure that he had ships going to Texas, Castro intensified his campaign to arrange matters there. He sent a number of dispatches, all very optimistic in tone. In them he emphasized the high quality of the colonists he was sending and indicated that the Texas government could expect at least one ship each month between November, 1842, and March, 1843. Because of his many difficulties, he requested a one-year extension of his contract. Then he tried to make some arrangement for the government to protect the colonists already en route to Texas. He repeatedly emphasized that, although he had provided as best he could for the immigrants, the republic should assume responsibility for their care and safety once they actually arrived in Texas. This would have the added benefit of insuring a continued immigration of French colonists to Texas that could easily reach into the thousands.[15]

Castro expressed particular concern with the location of his concession that had been crossed by the Mexican forces that invaded Texas during September. Therefore, he requested that the Texas government grant his colonists other lands away from the frontier so long as the proposed new grant was not in a fever-ridden section of the republic. Anson Jones understood the problems facing Castro in regard

[14] Anson Jones to Castro, January 4, 1843, Castro to Anson Jones, February 20, 1843, Colonization Papers; Although both Castro and Jones were convinced the letters never arrived, the missing letters appear in Garrison, *Correspondence*, II: 1375–79, where they are addressed to Ashbel Smith who was in Paris at the time. It must be assumed that the letters were not forwarded to Texas until a later date.

[15] Castro to Anson Jones, October 15, 1842, February 20, 1843, Colonization Papers; Castro to Anson Jones, November 15, 1842, Texas, Department of State Copybooks, 201–202.

to the grant location, but he also knew that the property request could not be acted on because the republic lacked available public lands in its more settled eastern regions. As a compromise Jones suggested to Castro that he should purchase property within the settlements where the immigrants could farm ten or fifteen acres each until the frontier region was safe. In this way they could familiarize themselves with Texas weather and agricultural practices. When it became safe to move onto the concession, the colonists would be ready to start their new lives and Castro would have no problem recouping his investment on the temporary property, which would have been considerably improved in the interim.[16]

While attempting to get the Republic of Texas to assume responsibility for the colonists, Castro continued his recruiting activities. By April, 1843, he had signed an additional seventy-six contracts that committed 240 people to leave for Texas that autumn. Many of the potential settlers were bachelors whom Castro felt should be allowed a family man's share of land providing they married after becoming colonists, but before the concession contract lapsed. In a letter to the secretary of state, the empresario argued that this policy would create an incentive for immigration as well as establishing a stable family-oriented population beneficial to the Republic of Texas.[17]

Meanwhile, vessels bearing the first colonists began to arrive in Texas. The Europeans definitely were not prepared for what they found. They had left a region of heavy population that contained numerous cities of considerable size. Moreover, few of them had ever traveled more than a few miles from their home prior to leaving for Texas. They found their new homeland to be a sparsely populated country of vast distances with few towns, none of which contained a population exceeding 3,000. Galveston, the port of call for the emigrant ships in 1843, was described by the French consul as

---

[16] Castro to Anson Jones, November 15, 1842, Texas, Department of State Copybooks, 201–202; Anson Jones to Castro, April 1, 1843, Colonization Papers.
[17] Castro to Anson Jones, April 1, 1843, Colonization Papers.

. . . a tiny city of approximately 1,500 people located on a bare and arid sand bar, exposed to the ravages of hurricanes and flood-waters of the Gulf. Only last September 8 a storm submerged the entire place, destroyed several buildings—in particular an unfin-ished church—and nearly washed away the whole city including its inhabitants. But this location has for foreigners, at least the ad-vantage of more or less regular communication with the outside world. . . .[18]

Despite its appearance, however, others ranked Galveston a metropolis when compared with nearby Houston which, de-spite a population nearing 3,000, seemed nothing more than a mass of muddy streets lined with disreputable unpainted buildings.[19]

The reaction of the *Ebro* passengers typified the feelings of those who followed. They arrived off Galveston on New Year's Day 1843, but were not allowed to disembark until January 9. In Galveston they learned that they would leave on the fifteenth by a coastal vessel for Lavaca Bay, a voyage of some fifty miles. From there they were scheduled to proceed overland by oxcart to San Antonio, a journey of some 150 miles. This revelation dismayed and confused the immi-grants who had assumed that upon arriving in Texas they had only to claim their land and begin a new life. It never occurred to them that they would have to travel tremendous distances through an unfamiliar countryside before arriving on the concession. Immediately five or six families refused to make the trip to San Antonio. Instead, they went to Houston with all its discomforts to await developments rather than en-dure further travel.[20]

The main party continued to San Antonio. Its members suffered tremendous hardships because the swampy coastal terrain caused the unwieldy oxcarts to bog down almost con-tinuously. They traveled at a snail's pace during the first leg of the land journey, only making three or four miles per day.

[18] Cramayel to Guizot, June 25, 1843, in Barker, *Legation*, II: 449.

[19] Francis S. Latham, *Travels in the Republic of Texas, 1842*, Gerald S. Pierce, ed., 34–35.

[20] Jean Marie Odin, Journal, 1842–1852. Typescript in Catholic Archives, Diocese of Galveston-Houston, Houston.

Many of the colonists developed fevers in the unhealthy coastal region prior to arriving at their destination. At San Antonio they found a partially deserted town of some 1,500 to 2,000 inhabitants, mostly Hispanic. The narrow streets of the town were lined with whitewashed one-story adobe structures, many of which had been abandoned during the recent war scare. To increase their misery further the immigrants discovered that they could not take possession of their lands, which lay less than fifty miles to the west, because of the unsettled nature of the frontier situation. Thus the unfortunate colonists were forced to remain in San Antonio and await their fate.[21]

As succeeding vessels arrived, most of the colonists also made their way as best they could to San Antonio in an attempt to take possession of their lands. This remained impossible because government officials refused to assume the responsibility of settling the immigrants on the exposed frontier. Faced with the prospect of waiting until something could be arranged, the unfortunate colonists were forced to rely upon their own resources or what they could secure from local residents in order to survive. President Houston attempted to help by issuing an order that allowed the colonists to occupy vacant structures within San Antonio. This did not altogether solve the housing dilemma, however, for many of the families either camped along the San Antonio River or lived in such unlikely places as the ruins of the Alamo mission. These unhealthy conditions in combination with the rigors of the journey proved fatal to several colonists, and practically all of them became ill with one malady or another.[22]

Not all the immigrants attempted to go immediately to San Antonio. For example, six *Ebro* families refused to make the first trip in January of 1843. Particularly after word of

---

[21] Latham, *Travels*, 34–35; Fretelliere, "Adventures," 15–20.

[22] Cramayel to Guizot, June 25, July 17, September 5, December 12, 1843, and March 8, 1844, in Barker, *Legation*, II: 449, 452–55, 470, 488, 506; Sam Houston to Maj. George T. Howard, January 24, 1842, in Williams and Barker, *Writings*, III: 440–41. The date on this letter is undoubtedly incorrect when stated as 1842 because Castro's contract was signed in February of 1842 and colonists did not arrive until January of 1843, therefore the correct date should be January 24, 1843; Bollaert, *Texas*, 221, 230, 347.

the situation of the San Antonio residents became common knowledge, more and more refused to go there. Some remained in Galveston or Houston and tried to find work. Others, if they had money, either returned to France or bought property in places such as Galveston, Houston, or Victoria and settled down to await developments. Whatever their financial circumstance, these colonists on the first three vessels arriving in Texas faced a dismal situation in their new homeland.[23]

While the colonists languished in Texas, Castro continued his recruiting activities in Europe. The destitute situation of the colonists already in Texas created problems for him, however, with both France and Texas. The Texas secretary of state charged that Castro was sending destitute immigrants who quickly became disgruntled with both Texas and the empresario, thereby causing problems for the republic. Jones emphasized that all persons going to Texas must have the means to live for one year, and those who did not should be discouraged from emigrating. At the same time, the French chargé d'affaires to Texas in his reports described in graphic detail the terrible condition of Castro colonists then residing in Texas and charged that the twenty-dollar fee paid by the colonists was the main object of the entire scheme. He believed that Castro intended to pocket the fee and allow the colonists to languish in Texas without getting any of the promised land. This information led Foreign Minister Guizot to recommend that Castro be stopped from recruiting in France.[24]

While he put pressure on Castro to cease operations, Guizot gave an excellent recommendation for the Bourgeois and Ducos colonization program. He emphasized that France should support honorable men like Bourgeois and Ducos even though they were recruiting French citizens to move to

[23] Fretelliere, "Adventures," 15; Ihnken File, Wurzbach File, Menke Collection; Bollaert, *Texas*, 347.

[24] Ashbel Smith to Anson Jones, June 16, 1843, Anson Jones to Ashbel Smith, June 21, 1843, in Garrison, *Correspondence*, II: 1449, 1452; Cramayel to Guizot, January 26, 1843, Guizot to Minister of Interior, March 20, 1843, Guizot to Cramayel, April 21, 1843, in Barker, *Legation*, II: 401–402, 416, 425.

a place that could not offer them the best protection or financial stability. Guizot favored Bourgeois over Castro primarily because he felt that Castro's scheme was fraudulent while he was confident Bourgeois would put colonists in possession of the lands as promised.[25]

Because of this unfortunate reaction to his efforts Castro changed the emphasis of his recruitment. He began the project in 1842 with Paris as the center of his activities and recruited many of the colonists from the vicinity of Paris and such interior French departments as Marne. True, many of the first colonists did come from Alsace and the Swiss border, but they embarked from the French ports of Le Havre and Dunquerque. With the resumption of shipping activities in the fall of 1843, practically all of the colonists came from Alsace, the Swiss border, or the neighboring German states and embarked from the Belgian port of Antwerp.[26]

This change in recruiting area was made due to several circumstances. Experienced farmers who were renting their land were available in Alsace and neighboring areas, which made that region a likely place to find recruits, but at least as important was the strong opposition of the French government. That opposition apparently stemmed from the unfavorable reports on Castro's character, although the empresario maintained that it was because of the official French policy that directed all emigration toward Algeria. Regardless of the reason, by recruiting in the northeastern corner of France, Castro kept his activities some distance from the seat of power in Paris, which enabled him to act with somewhat less restraint than if he were in a place where the officials could watch him closely.[27]

By concentrating his operation in the Alsace region, Castro made perhaps one of the most fortunate moves of his

[25] Cramayel to Guizot, January 26, 1843, Guizot to Minister of Interior, February 16, March 20, 1843, in Barker, *Legation*, II: 401–402, 412, 416.

[26] Ships' Lists for *Ebro, Lyons, Louis Philippe, Jean Key,* and *Henrich,* Colonization Papers.

[27] Ludwig Huth to Louis Huth, November 20, 1843, Castro to Louis Huth, December 1, 1843, Ferdinand Louis Huth Papers, Barker Texas History Center, University of Texas at Austin; Ashbel Smith to Anson Jones December 1, 1843, Colonization Papers.

colonization effort. During the summer or early fall of 1843 he first made contact with the Huth family, whose members were to be instrumental in making his program success-ful. Ludwig Huth was a well-to-do merchant and insurance company owner in Neufreystaedt, Baden, just across the Rhine from the French department of Bas Rhin. Well-known and respected in business circles of the region, Huth made an excellent contact for recruiting colonists for the Texas concession.[28]

Huth and Castro established a business arrangement that seemed advantageous to both parties. The agreement, signed early in October, 1843, established a partnership whereby Ludwig's eldest son, Ferdinand Louis, would travel to Texas to act as both a manager of colonization and a business agent. Castro agreed to furnish 12,000 francs ($2,400) in goods to be transported to Texas on emigrant vessels. In Texas, Louis was to trade or sell the goods and ship cotton, hides, or other salable goods back to either Amsterdam, Antwerp, or Le Havre, where his father would dispose of them at favorable prices. The profits from the venture were to be divided equally between Huth and Company, Louis Huth, and Cas-tro. The initial arrangement was to last for two years, after which it would be continued on a shipment-by-shipment basis. Additionally, the Huths were to receive 10,000 acres of land in the colony for Louis acting as Castro's agent in Texas. Thus at one stroke the empresario solved the problem of a responsible agent in Texas, arranged for a return cargo on emigrant vessels, and added an impetus to his European re-cruiting efforts.[29]

To assist in the financial agreement with the Huth family Castro asked the Texas government to give him duty-free status on goods shipped to Texas on emigrant vessels. He claimed that beginning in 1844 all arriving vessels would have at least 120 colonists aboard who would each have 1,500

[28] "History of Some German Pioneer Families and Their Part in the Develop-ment and Colonization of Texas: Three Generations of Huths," *Texas Centennial Magazine*, March, 1936, 10.
[29] Contract between Ludwig Huth, Ferdinand Louis Huth, and Henri Castro, October 5, 1843, Power of Attorney in Texas from Henri Castro to Louis Huth, Oc-tober 15, 1843, Huth Papers.

francs ($300) plus sufficient tools and clothing to establish them in their new environment. He proposed that the republic allow him duty-free 100,000 francs ($20,000) worth of merchandise on each ship. He had a franchise on these goods from Belgian manufacturers who agreed to maintain the requisite number and quality of colonists on each vessel. He emphasized that in return for his duty-free status, the republic would greatly increase its population and promote commerce at one stroke.[30]

The Huths wasted little time getting involved in the operation. Louis left for Texas from Antwerp aboard the *Jean Key* on October 23, 1843, accompanied by 128 other passengers, fifty of whom were eligible to receive land grants. For the first time the immigrants included Germans from Baden and Nassau as well as several Swiss colonists. The overwhelming bulk of the passengers were Alsatians, however, from Haut and Bas Rhin. Once again the evidence indicates that this group of colonists was virtually without funds. The *Jean Key* was followed a month later by the *Henrich* which left Strasbourg by way of Antwerp bound for Galveston. Although the *Henrich* ship's list is incomplete, the place of origin for the 136 immigrants whose names appear is virtually the same as for those on the *Jean Key*. The two groups differed primarily in that all the families on the *Henrich* declared property—in some instances considerable amounts.[31]

At this point a hiatus appears in the departure of vessels because another ship transporting Castro colonists did not leave for Texas until April, 1844. The reason is not readily evident, but probably the French government had some success in slowing down recruitment. When the *Ocean* left Antwerp on the ninth of April she carried ninety colonists, forty-one of whom were eligible to receive land, including twenty-two bachelors. For the first time numerous Swiss were included in the company, while the rest of the group came from the German states, Holland, and Alsace. This vessel

[30] Castro to Anson Jones, October 25, 1843, Colonization Papers.

[31] Ship's Lists for the *Jean Key* (Louis Huth who declared 20,000 francs was the only passenger to declare any property at all) and the *Henrich*, Colonization Papers; Castro to Louis Huth, December 1, 1843, Huth Papers; this letter indicated that there were 140 passengers on the *Henrich* instead of the 136 listed on the ship's list.

included a rather unusual party of eighteen persons from Prussia who pooled 20,000 francs ($4,000) to make the voyage. The passengers aboard the *Ocean*, like those on the *Henrich*, seem to have been in fairly good financial circumstances although six families listed no property at all. The *Ocean* was followed on May 12 by the *Jeanette Marie* from Antwerp with only thirty-nine passengers representing fourteen potential landholders. This particular group came entirely from Haut and Bas Rhin except for one individual from Holland. Financially they were in poor circumstances, although Castro highly recommended them as "brave and honest men who are excellent farmers."[32]

When Louis Huth arrived in Texas late in December he was appalled by the situation he found there. No Castro agent met him in Galveston despite the empresario's assurance that he and the colonists accompanying him would be cared for by competent representatives. He discovered that the plight of the colonists was much worse than he imagined, and that he must render immediate aid to them if he could. Further, the chances for commerce appeared less bright than they might have been—the *Louis Philippe* had recently sailed back to France with only ballast in her hold after delivering the colonists she had transported.[33]

Meanwhile, Castro wrote apologizing for the poor quality of the colonists sent in the past, but promising a better class of people in the future. He advised Louis not to economize on expenses, but to aid the colonists in anyway he could. Castro particularly wanted Huth to proceed to San Antonio as soon as possible, lend corn to the needy until the next harvest, and build them sheds until cabins could be constructed. Further, he assured Louis that he had made business arrangements in Europe that would materially assist them in their business venture.[34]

The elder Huth, eager to get their business venture underway, sent on the *Henrich* 100,000 francs ($20,000), which he was sure would return a handsome profit when invested

[32] Ships' Lists for the *Ocean* and *Jeanette Marie*, Colonization Papers.
[33] August Huth to Louis Huth, April 7, 1844, Huth Papers; Cramayel to Guizot, December 28, 1843, Barker, *Legation*, II: 491.
[34] Castro to Louis Huth, November 15, December 1, 1843, Huth Papers.

in Texas cotton. The old man became excited about getting the several thousand acres promised by Castro, for there seemed little doubt in his mind that the Huth family had practically made its fortune. He also emphasized that they would be sending a better class of immigrants in the future, but he warned Louis to keep on deposit all land contracts as security until the colonists repaid their loans for passage to Texas.[35]

By the spring of 1844 Castro's colonization program was assuming an aura of professionalism. Beginning with the acquisition of the concession in February, 1842, the empresario worked diligently to make the program a reality. Perhaps he proceeded too rapidly by sending unqualified colonists, but he felt a great deal of pressure to qualify his contract by getting a minimum of 200 potential landholders in Texas during the first eighteen months. In fairness to Castro, it should be pointed out that he thought the Texas government would assume some of the responsibility for getting the colonists settled on their lands, when in fact that never occurred.

The problems of unsettled conditions in Texas, opposition to the project in France, and competition from the Bourgeois interests created almost insurmountable obstacles to Castro's program. Nevertheless, he continued to recruit and send colonists to Texas. By mid-1843 it became obvious that the organization needed a better means of administration. At this point the Huth family assumed a position of importance in the program.

During the winter of 1843 Castro solved some of his greatest problems. The Huth agreement gave an added income dimension to the enterprise. At the same time the elder Huth in Europe could recruit colonists, while his son, Louis, assumed the responsibility of coordinating events in Texas. Thus, at the beginning of 1844 the colonization program assumed the sound basis that would ultimately carry it through to completion.

---

[35] Ludwig Huth to Louis Huth, November 24, December 26, 1843, March, 1844, and May, 1844, Huth Papers.

CHAPTER III

A Town Is Founded

THE spring of 1844 brought new life to the colonization project when Henri Castro returned to Texas. Although more than 200 potential settlers already were in the republic, no colonist had taken possession of his property. Indeed, most of the colonists remained in San Antonio in a state of abject poverty, ruing the day that they had left Europe. Castro realized that he must take a personal hand in Texas to get his people on concession land or the project would fail. With this thought in mind, the empresario made arrangements to leave Europe and establish his first settlement.

Castro departed Europe from Liverpool, England, on May 19, aboard the steamship *Caledonia*, rather than going by one of the slower sail-powered emigrant vessels. Coincidentally, Bourgeois d'Orvanne embarked aboard the same vessel. Bourgeois traveled with Prince Carl of Solms-Braunfels and a large entourage. This enforced close relationship aboard ship must have been somewhat uncomfortable considering the extreme rivalry between the two men in recruiting European citizens for their adjoining concessions in Texas. Both groups retraced Castro's route to Texas in 1842 and arrived in New Orleans on June 14 after a tiring overland trip in unaccustomed summer heat.[1]

Perhaps the relative success of Castro's efforts at recruit-

[1] Henri Castro, Journal, Barker Texas History Center, University of Texas at Austin; Castro to Anson Jones, May 12, 1844, Colonization Papers, Archives, Texas State Library, Austin; Ashbel Smith to Anson Jones, May 6, 1844, George P. Garrison, ed., *Diplomatic Correspondence of the Republic of Texas*, II: 1484.

ing colonists can be better understood when compared to the efforts of his unexpected traveling companion. The Bourgeois contract, issued only four months after Castro's, represented essentially the same instrument in a similar part of the country. Bourgeois had the additional responsibility of selling Republic of Texas bonds worth one million dollars; for these, however, Cherokee lands in East Texas were held as security. Although he did establish a colonization company, Compagnie Générale de Colonisation au Texas, and advertise for colonists, Bourgeois never made any serious effort to settle the concession. Instead, he spent most of his time trying to interest other European groups in his project so that they could invest their money and take all the risks while he would share in any profits. Meanwhile most of his efforts were aimed at getting the million-dollar loan arranged either with or without the colonization program being involved.[2]

This explains why Bourgeois was on his way to Texas. He had managed to interest a group of German investors in the project and Prince Carl of Solms-Braunfels was accompanying him to Texas as representative of their Society for the Protection of German Immigrants in Texas.[3]

The investors had agreed to finance the colonization scheme and to look into the bond loan as a joint investment project. By contrast, Castro assumed full financial and personal involvement in his concession. He recruited his own colonists and financed the entire operation, which entailed far more risk, but at the same time his potential profits were much greater.

Meanwhile, both parties stayed at the St. James Hotel in New Orleans. During their sojourn there, both received invi-

[2] Thomas W. Streeter, *Bibliography of Texas, 1795–1845*, III: 411; Sam Houston to House of Representatives, January 27, 1844, in Amelia W. Williams and Eugene C. Barker, eds., *The Writings of Sam Houston*, IV: 235; Anson Jones to Ashbel Smith, December 26, 1842, September 30, 1843, Anson Jones to Bourgeois d'Orvanne, December 26, 1842, Ashbel Smith to Anson Jones, October 15, October 21, 1842, March 31, April 11, June 16, 1843, and February 26, 1844, in Garrison, *Correspondence*, II: 1410, 1141, 1410, 1384, 1390, 1428, 1433, 1450, 1481.

[3] For a complete account of Bourgeois d'Orvanne's association with the Society for the Protection of German Immigrants, see Rudolph Biesele, *The History of German Settlements in Texas*, 66–67.

tations to dine at the home of a wealthy New Orleans merchant named Lanfear. Castro took advantage of the social gathering to present to Bourgeois a plan of cooperation between their respective colonization efforts. Solms expressed interest in the proposal, but Bourgeois strongly opposed any sort of partnership. This effectively blocked Castro's attempt to diminish competition from another empresario and intensified the antipathy between him and Bourgeois.

On July 3 Castro finally set foot on Texas soil at Galveston. News of his return had preceded him, and an angry crowd of disappointed colonists met him at the waterfront demanding the return of their deposits. The empresario evidently had expected trouble and had secreted two pistols on his person in case matters became too violent. Force proved unnecessary, however, as the glib-tongued promoter explained away delays and inability to take possession of concession lands as being the fault of unreliable agents. Ultimately, he convinced the bulk of the people of his sincerity, although he was forced to return deposits to an adamant few.

Louis Huth arrived in Galveston to report to Castro. The report confirmed what Castro fully suspected: the situation in Texas was very unsatisfactory indeed. For the first time, he discovered the extent of the money spent on the project and how few were the tangible results of the efforts. The colonists had reached San Antonio in large numbers, as he knew. But he had not known that they had virtually no protection and that none of them had been able to take possession of their lands, which lay only thirty miles to the west. To make matters worse, Huth, like many of the other colonists, had become ill with "the fever" and could not assist Castro at the time.[4]

Undaunted, the empresario left Galveston on July 4 by steamboat for Houston. There he traveled around in a splendidly furnished carriage recently purchased to create a favorable impression on the Texans. During one of his first calls the Catholic Bishop, Jean Marie Odin, gave his official

---

[4]Castro, Journal, 89–91.

approval of the colonization project, influenced no doubt by receiving 1,100 francs from Castro in repayment of money the bishop had advanced to some unfortunate colonists the previous year. During their visit Castro learned that Bourgeois and Solms-Braunfels had been there on a similar mission the preceding day, but already had left to meet with Sam Houston at Washington-on-the-Brazos.[5]

Fearing that Bourgeois might gain a political advantage over him, Castro followed the next day. Fortunately he gave Washington Miller, Sam Houston's personal secretary, a ride in the new coach. The trip proved very difficult for the Frenchman newly arrived on the frontier because of flooding in the Brazos "bottoms" and the oppressive heat, which hovered around ninety-five degrees. On the seventh they arrived in Washington, where they found Solms-Braunfels and Bourgeois creating quite an impression with a retinue of some ten or twelve retainers dressed in livery and acting every bit the part of European royalty.

Castro discovered almost immediately that the president was out of town, but when the oppressive heat abated late that afternoon, he paid a visit to Secretary of State Anson Jones at his farm a few miles outside of town. The meeting with Jones proved to be very fruitful. The secretary of state assured Castro that his contract was safe, although all others had been canceled in accordance with a recently passed law that required all concession contracts be ended unless the empresarios involved had complied strictly with the stipulations of their contracts. He emphasized that this action stemmed directly from the fact that Texans were concerned about European immigrants, who seemed to exhibit a definite opposition to slavery. Castro managed to convince Jones that his colonists represented no particular opposition to slavery and thus posed no threat to existing Texas institutions. The empresario left his meeting with Jones completely

---

[5] Ibid., 91; Odin to Etienne, January 13, 1843, Odin to Rousselan, October 1, 1843, Odin to Etienne, January 23, 1843, Jean Marie Odin, Papers, Catholic Archives of Texas, Austin; Jean Marie Odin, Journal, 1842–43, typescript, Diocesan Records, Diocese of Galveston-Houston, Houston, January 25, 1843, July 3, 1844.

reassured that his rapid colonization efforts, although unfortunate for the unprepared colonists, had saved the concession from being canceled.[6]

The two-hundred-mile trip from Washington to San Antonio took a full week. Castro, accompanied only by the faithful Huth, suffered tremendously from the heat, which continued unabated. His arrival in San Antonio was met with less than unbounded enthusiasm. As in Galveston, the colonists flocked to him and poured out their grievances, demanding some sort of restitution. This continued until after nightfall when the beleaguered Castro at last found some relief by securing lodging with a friendly Italian, Locmar Antonio.[7]

The next day, July 19, Castro promulgated the first of several rousing proclamations designed to reassure the colonists and get the project moving. He reminded them that only through his efforts had they received the opportunity to get free land at all. He promised to take care of their families and support them in every way until they were safe on their properties. In short, he told them everything he could think of to keep them involved in the project, including the promise of large numbers of new arrivals who would soon join them and assist in the work.

It is doubtful that the proclamation had a significant effect in changing anyone's attitude, but Castro realized that positive action must be taken and soon. Accordingly, he left on July 25 to inspect concession lands, accompanied by five men provided by the secretary of war from Captain Jack Hays's Ranger Company, as well as seven others, including John James, deputy surveyor for Bexar County. The party traveled well armed because of the recent escalation of Indian sightings in the area.

On the morning of July 27, 1844, they crossed the Medina River and four miles to the west Castro entered for the

---

[6]Castro, Journal, 91–93; Castro to Paris Friends, July 9, 1844, Castro, Journal, 95–96; Castro to Sam Houston, July 9, 1844, Colonization Papers; H. P. N. Gammel, *The Laws of Texas 1822–1897*, II: 46–47.

[7]Castro, Journal, July 12–18, 1844, 104; Saligny to Guizot, September 28, 1844, Nancy Nichols Barker, ed., *The French Legation in Texas*, II, 572.

first time the concession land he had contracted for over two years before. Soon after the inspection began, the empresario found an impressive site for a town on the banks of Quihi Lake nine or ten miles west of the Medina River. This location had plenty of wood, water, and fertile soil that suited his needs perfectly. As the inspection proceeded, he located another potential settlement site still farther west on the banks of Hondo Creek. After viewing in some detail this northern portion of the grant, which was well suited to colonization, the party returned by way of Quihi Lake. Once again Castro commented favorably on the settlement possibilities of that location, which included permanent water and an abundance of fish and game. At that time there seemed little doubt that he intended to make his first permanent settlement on Quihi Lake.

The party arrived back in San Antonio the last day of July, 1844, to find that things had not gone well in their absence. Bourgeois, Solms-Braunfels and company had arrived in town the very day that Castro left on his inspection tour. Contrary to what Castro had understood on his Washington visit, Bourgeois and his group still believed that they had an excellent chance to retain and settle their concession, which joined Castro's on the north and west. Accordingly, they had been entertaining the Castro colonists in San Antonio during the empresario's absence, offering them an interesting alternative to their original settlement intention. Many of the original Castro people already had agreed to join the Solms-Braunfels group. Castro became furious and blamed Bourgeois and a German named Rump, who belonged to Hays's Ranger Company, as the main instigators of the defection.

To counteract the recruiting activities of the other Europeans, Castro issued another proclamation to the colonists. In it he introduced several inducements for settling on his concession. After describing the fertile land around Quihi Lake where the first settlement would be established, he promised a free house to each colonist to be constructed by common labor with Castro furnishing all food for the colonists until the homes were completed. Next, he promised to supply enough cows to furnish milk for one year and in addi-

tion beeves and ploughs to those without the means to provide them. Those without any money were promised enough
corn, bacon, and salt to tide them over until they made their
first crop. Finally, he promised to pay the colonists a wage
commensurate with their abilities for laboring to establish
the colony.[8]

Further complications arose when Prince Carl found
that John McMullen of San Antonio possessed sixteen leagues
of land adjoining Castro's concession on the east. The prince
consulted with McMullen about purchasing the property,
which would allow him to bracket the Castro grant as well as
giving the German a staging area for his proposed colony.
Before completing the deal, Solms-Braunfels left on an inspection tour of the property to decide if he actually wanted
to purchase it.[9]

When he heard of the proposed McMullen deal, Castro
was horrified. If the proposition was completed, he would be
ruined. There seemed little hope he could compete with a
project that held land closer to San Antonio than his own.
With that thought in mind, he approached McMullen about
buying the land. Within two days they put together a complicated land-purchase scheme that effectively blocked any-
thing the prince might try. The McMullen deal, completed
on August 23, 1844, was an involved business arrangement.
Basically, it stipulated that the sixteen leagues of land known
as the McMullen Grant could be used by Castro to settle his
colonists. The empresario agreed to establish one or more
towns on the property. If within two years he had a sufficient
number of people living on the land, he would receive title to
one-half the grant. Compensation to McMullen would be
$2,000, payable at the end of two years. Castro's portion of
the grant consisted of the northern half, which abutted on
his concession opposite the site of Quihi and included front-
age on both sides of the Medina River.[10]

[8]Proclamation, July 19, 1844, and Proclamation, August 12, 1844, Castro,
Journal, 106–109.

[9]Castro, Journal, 108; Carl of Solms-Braunfels, *Texas 1844–1845*, trans. unknown, 45.

[10]Castro, Journal, 108; Deed Records, County Clerk's Office, Bexar County
Courthouse, San Antonio, Book B2, 293, Book C2, 5.

As soon as he completed the property arrangement with McMullen, Castro changed the entire thrust of his settlement program. The first indication of this came in an August 20 proclamation to his colonists. Feeling secure now that he had blocked the latest attempts against his colonization efforts, Castro opened with charges of base intrigues against his project, while emphasizing that he had been open and honest in his dealings. To prove his sincerity, the empresario described his acquisition of the McMullen land some ten miles nearer San Antonio than the concession property. To each colonist who followed him to the concession he promised forty acres plus a town lot, free of charge, to be located within the confines of the newly purchased lands. This grant was to be in addition to the 320 acres for family heads and 160 acres for bachelors already due to colonists on concession land. He emphasized that this new liberality greatly surpassed his contract with the colonists and they would be wise to appreciate its value.

Once he put forth the new inducement to the colonists, Castro began an intensive campaign to get all of them enrolled to follow him. He indicated again and again the advantages of staying associated with the enterprise. The empresario warned them that, while he understood their feelings, they were receiving bad advice. He promised that he would bear no animosity toward anyone provided he continued to follow his example. He claimed to have a list of fifty who would follow him immediately, and the fall of 1844 and the spring of 1845 would see thousands more arriving from Europe.

The colonists faced a decision when on August 23 Castro sent a personal letter to each. He informed them that he would leave San Antonio on Saturday, August 31, to occupy colony lands that individual colonists were supposed to share. If they planned to be a part of that activity, they must sign up on the twenty-seventh or the twenty-eighth.[11]

On the same day Castro learned another good piece of

[11] Proclamation, August 20, 1844, Castro, Journal, 111–12. In this proclamation the land promised the colonists is one-half that indicated in the law, which is the amount the colonists would receive after paying Castro his half.

news. Prince Carl received word from Europe that the Society for the Protection of German Immigrants had cancelled the Bourgeois agreement. The prince was to break off all relations with Bourgeois and travel immediately to the coast where he would meet Henry Fisher and Burchard Miller, with whom the society had negotiated for a different grant farther to the north. Castro was delighted. He reveled in the news and took every opportunity to ridicule the hapless Bourgeois, who was forced to remain in San Antonio for sometime because of the danger from a yellow-fever epidemic that was raging in Galveston. Now the way appeared clear for Castro to proceed without concern over so great a rival.[12]

With the threat of the Bourgeois grant gone, Castro began to apply more pressure to the recalcitrant colonists. On August 30 he issued yet another proclamation in which he stated that those who were with him when he took possession of the land would receive a free house built with common labor. If they came later and arrived prior to September 15 they would get a town lot, but would have to build their own house. After September 15 contracts of absent colonists would be irrevocably annulled.

Meanwhile, factors uncontrollable by Castro affected the project. A group of colonists who left Galveston early in July met delays caused by sickness. Additionally, a nineteen-year-old member of that same convoy, Ziliax Rhin, was killed by unknown Indians. The incident transpired at the Santitas Ranch, only forty miles from San Antonio, when the cart Rhin was riding in fell behind the rest of the convoy and was attacked by twenty Indians. The Texan driver managed to escape, but poor Rhin was killed and later his severed hand was found nailed to a nearby tree. The Indians' presence aroused concern again when on August 26 tribesmen stole eleven mules from an enclosure less than two hundred yards

[12]Castro, Journal, 114; Henry F. Fisher to Anson Jones, March 12, June 27, 1844, *Charles*, Prince of Solms-Braunfels to Anson Jones, November 2, 1844, in Anson Jones, *Memoranda and Official Correspondence Relating to the Republic of Texas*. Fifth Congress, First Session, 326, 367, 391–92; William Kennedy to Addington, October 24, 1844, in Ephraim Douglass Adams, ed., *British Diplomatic Correspondence Concerning the Republic of Texas*, 372; Saligny to Guizot, August 12, August 27, 1844, in Barker, *Legation*, II: 558, 566–67; Odin, Journal, 32.

from Castro's residence on Soledad Street. No wonder the immigrants felt intimidated and frightened—death and disease seemed to threaten them at every turn in an alien environment they did not understand.

The obviously negative attitude of the colonists caused the empresario to redouble his efforts to start the settlement convoy off on the appointed day. Then another totally unexpected source of opposition came to light. The business element in San Antonio opposed the establishment of the colony. The formation of a town to the west posed a threat to the control of trade with Mexico by San Antonio. Furthermore, the continued residence of the colonists in town provided a cheap labor pool for the local business community. The businessmen began to circulate rumors of greater Indian depredations and of imminent fall rains that would hamper the construction of new homes, and ultimately threatened colonists with loss of the jobs that provided their only income. All these rumors prompted Castro to accept only men for his initial sortie onto the concession. He promised that the families remaining in San Antonio during the interim would be provided for until it was safe to move them west.

The appointed day for leaving San Antonio neared and Castro managed to get all in readiness. On Saturday, August 31, he invited all the colonists designated to go with him, along with their families and some American friends, to attend a gala party celebrating the beginning of the grand enterprise. As the evening wore on and the drinks flowed freely, a spirit of goodwill pervaded the gathering, with numerous toasts made to the success of the endeavor.

The next morning at four o'clock Castro had twenty-two carts prepared for loading and all the gear to make the trip in readiness. Gradually it became apparent that he would not be able to leave with fifty men as he had boasted. In fact, he could muster fewer than half that number. The colonists' fear of striking out into the unknown, which had been heightened by rumors of Indian problems, was not improved by the dreary, wet weather. Castro sent messengers all over town to rouse the laggards. They came but usually with some lame excuse or promises of later support. To increase interest he

kept an open table all day loaded with meat and drink. By
two o'clock in the afternoon heavy rain poured down and
Castro had managed to muster only twenty-seven colonists,
augmented by twelve Mexican cart drivers he had hired by
paying excessively high wages. This bedraggled group left
San Antonio at four o'clock in the afternoon on September 1,
1844, traveling in eleven carts through a driving rain bound
for the Medina River to found the first town of Castro's
colony.[13]

The expedition reached the Medina the following day
and Castro reconnoitered the area to find a suitable spot to
establish a town. He picked a location on the west side of the
river in a bight made by the river curving sharply to the east.
Next morning the entire company crossed the river at a ford
located about midway of the eastward curve in the river. The
group found themselves in a level parklike area covered with
pecan trees. Declaring this to be the site of his first town in
Texas, Castro had hot meals served and provided plenty of
free liquor for his assembled men. This brought the first
day's activities on the site of the new town to a congenial
end.[14]

The group that gathered that day on the Medina did not
altogether represent those who had suffered so in San Antonio. Among them stood Theodore Gentilz, an accomplished
artist from Paris whose artistic endeavors on the Texas frontier were to become well known. Dr. George Cupples, a Scot-
tish physician, later to gain fame as one of the founders of
the Texas Medical Association, also came there as a colonist.
Their guide and interpreter, Charles de Montel, had arrived
in Texas from Germany in 1836, and fought at the battle of
San Jacinto, where he changed his name from Scheidemontle
to de Montel. He was destined to become a substantial and
prominent citizen in the region. Many of the others would
become prosperous in their new homeland, a few would become average frontier settlers, and some would disappear
from the scene and be lost to history. These average settlers

[13] Castro, Journal, 113, 115–21; Odin, Journal, 32.
[14] Castro, Journal, 121–22.

included farmers, stonemasons, shoemakers, and a myriad of other workers who had arrived in Texas with few resources, facing an uncertain future.[15]

On September 5, John James arrived from San Antonio to begin the survey of Castroville and the forty-acre "out lots." Castro began to organize the labor situation reasonably, despite a major dispute between French and German colonists that he managed to settle amicably. By September 7 things seemed to be well enough in order for Cupples and de Montel to return to San Antonio and escort Bishop Odin to the site for the dedication of a proposed church.[16]

Since their original departure from San Antonio, the small body of colonists had felt considerable concern about the danger from Indians. Well aware of the potential danger, Castro took great pains to mount guards, but no problem developed. Then on September 9 one of the colonists reported finding the trail of fifty mounted Comanches, and the ever-present danger of Indian attack struck fear in the hearts of the Europeans. They immediately built a strong guard house and Castro sent for Captain Hays and his rangers to provide more protection.[17]

The following day Cupples and de Montel arrived from San Antonio with Bishop Odin and Rev. Jules Oge. Captain Hays also appeared on the scene to review the Indian scare, which he dismissed as insignificant. Work began at this time on a large shed with a thatched roof to give the men a shelter for sleeping. The visitors were entertained and shown the progress made on the settlement. On September 12 Bishop Odin laid the cornerstone of the new church, which he dedicated in the name of St. Louis.[18]

Dedication day for the new church represented a mo-

[15] Dorothy Steinbomer Kendall, *Gentilz: Artist of the Old Southwest*, 4–49; Pat Ireland Nixon, *A Century of Medicine in San Antonio, Texas*, 168; J. Marvin Hunter, *One Hundred Years in Bandera, 1853–1953*, 5–6; DeMontel File, James Menke Collection, San Antonio; Survey of over 500 files on individuals associated with the Castro Colony, Menke Collection.

[16] Castro, Journal, 123.

[17] Castro to Anson Jones, August 19, September 6, October 6, 1844, Colonization Papers; Castro, Journal, 123.

[18] Castro, Journal, 124–25; Odin, Journal, 32.

mentous occasion for the colony. In addition to the religious
activities the colonists performed necessary secular duties. In
an election Louis Huth and G. S. Bourgeois won positions as
justices while Louis Haass became constable. After the election the newly formed settlement received the official name
Castroville in honor of the empresario. Thus the colony was
officially launched with both religious and legal formalities.[19]

In founding his first town, even though it did not stand
on concession land proper, Castro carefully had all participants sign documents attesting to the event. Bishop Odin,
for example, signed a statement attested to by the French
consul in San Antonio, F. Guilbeau, that he had dedicated
the church and that there were several colonists busily working at the site to form a permanent colony. John James also
signed a statement that he had surveyed concession lands assigned to those who accompanied Castro on the first trip to
establish Castroville. Then the twenty-seven colonists who
made the trip signed a document in which they outlined the
empresario's activities that had put them in possession of
their new property. They stated that they had received town
lots and were well satisfied with their situation in Texas. Thus
Castro armed himself with written verification to convince
scoffers that he had established his colony.[20]

Even though Castro had made a firm beginning with the
founding of Castroville, it remained necessary for him to
persuade the remaining colonists in Texas to join the new
settlement. With this in mind the empresario, along with
Huth and Cupples, accompanied Bishop Odin and Reverend
Oge back to San Antonio on September 13. There Castro
persuaded twenty colonists, mostly the families of men already at Castroville, to accompany his convoy of six carts
back to the newly established town. They left San Antonio in
a driving rain and experienced the same kind of weather that

[19]Castro, Journal, 125–27; Castro to Anson Jones, September 15, 1844, Colonization Papers. This letter is a report on all activities at Castroville through September 12.

[20]Affidavit of Jean Marie Odin, September 12, 1844, Affidavit of John James,
September 14, 1844, Process Verbal signed by the twenty-seven first colonists, September 12, 1844, Castro, Journal, 125, 128.

had plagued the earlier migrants until they reached the settlement three days later.

Meanwhile work on the settlement suffered. The heavy rain caused work to be suspended as the damp colonists huddled miserably beneath their makeshift shelters. Even with the arrival of the second convoy of settlers, the work went slowly. To complicate matters further, the considerable confusion of languages led the French, German, Texas, and Mexican workers to establish separate camps and refuse to cooperate with one another. Even though the inclement weather had dampened the enthusiasm for work, there was a plentiful supply of food, with deer, bear, and turkey slaughtered on a regular basis.

During this difficult period a colonist named Mercier became lost for three days. Upon his safe return he recited an exciting account of seeing Indians and living on muskrats the entire time. Indeed, adventures of this kind became a sort of game as the Europeans began to learn more about their new home. To many, especially the younger members, it seemed a great adventure; but to the serious family men and women it confirmed many of the rumors they had heard while living in San Antonio.

The problem of getting colonists to leave the relative safety of San Antonio and move to the settlement continued to plague Castro. The agents of Prince Carl, especially Rump, who seems to have been particularly persuasive, still worked to get the colonists to move to the prince's settlements. The third convoy destined for Castroville delayed leaving for two days as the uncertain colonists weighed the arguments of both Castro and the prince before continuing to the French concession as originally planned.[21]

Meanwhile, the rains continued and morale among the colonists deteriorated. The downpour that began on September 17 continued for almost two weeks. Tempers flared as the shelters in the settlement proved woefully inadequate. Unused to such trying circumstances, the French at one point

[21] Odin, Journal, 32; Castro, Journal, 131–32.

refused to mount guard, but Castro managed to head off the budding mutiny before it gained momentum. The only bright spots during this period came with the occasional visits of Captain Hays and his rangers, who camped on Medio Creek, just twelve miles east of Castroville.

Then on September 30 the sun came out, the temperature rose, and with it the spirits of the colonists. Work resumed with a will as the clearing of the town lots proceeded apace. However, amidst the rising spirits a moment of sadness occurred when little two-year-old August Haller died for lack of medicine in the camp. His death became the first recorded in Castroville, and undoubtedly reminded all the colonists of their isolated and vulnerable situation on the frontier.[22]

With the work going well and the colonists in general good spirits, Castro, escorted by Louis Huth and Louis Haass, made yet another visit to San Antonio to persuade more colonists to join those at Castroville. The empresario stayed there from the sixth through the tenth of October, working diligently to retain the loyalty of the colonists. During this time he almost lost fifteen settlers to Bourgeois d'Orvanne, who was still in town, but in the end Castro won out.

With the San Antonio situation well in hand and the good weather still holding, work on the settlement proceeded rapidly. Things seemed to be in such good condition that on October 13 Castro took twelve armed men with him and proceeded to Quihi Lake to decide on the exact location for his next town. While there he surveyed the site destined to be the first village actually on concession property.

Meanwhile, adventures continued to befall the newly arrived colonists. Game remained plentiful and exotic episodes such as the killing of a fifteen-foot alligator by some French settlers, created momentary diversions. Then on October 14 a settler named Menetrier had the misfortune to be accosted by four armed Mexican bandits who robbed him and set him afoot. Although the colonists instigated an immediate pursuit of the outlaws, they were unable to overtake them. On

[22]Odin, Journal, 32; Castro, Journal, 132–33.

October 17 the colonists experienced their first Texas norther, which lowered the temperature thirty degrees in two hours and caused all the settlers to build roaring fires in their several camps.

Construction continued at a brisk pace with the threat of cold weather in the offing. Finally, a revolt against mounting the guard each night broke out among the overworked settlers. Castro put the matter to a vote at a general assembly of those present and gave a strong reprimand to one of the ringleaders named Roilet. On November 11 the little settlement received a visit by a delegation of San Antonians, including the sheriff and county judge. The visitors stayed for two days and were so impressed that two of them bought lots in the town.[23]

By the middle of November, Castro had two houses completed for himself, one built of adobe brick and the other of wood. The wooden house stood amidst a three-acre plot designed to grow cotton, sugar cane, and European grains as well as grape vines and fruit arbors. The garden even produced some radishes that fall. In addition to the empresario's houses the homes of other colonists were either completed or nearing completion. By November 21 when Castro left his growing community to return to France, the settlement consisted of sixty-three family heads or single men, all of whom possessed forty-acre out lots on the east side of the Medina as well as lots within the town proper on the west side of the river.[24]

The year 1844 marks the pivotal point in Castro's colonization efforts. Prior to that time he had concentrated on providing the means to get the colonists to Texas and trying to get the republic to settle them on their lands. When it became obvious that the Texas government either could not or would not help him to any extent, he had to take personal

---

[23] Saligny to Guizot, November 12, 1844, in Barker, *Legation*, II: 581; Castro, Journal, 133–35.

[24] Castro, Journal, 136; Deed Records, Bexar County Clerk's Office, Book C2, 5; Odin to Blanc, December 10, 1844, Odin to Timon, December 11, 1844, Odin to Society for the Propagation of the Faith, April 9, 1847, Odin Papers, Catholic Archives of Texas, Austin.

command of the situation in Texas. By going to the concession and actually putting the colonists on or near their property, he greatly enhanced the chances of a successful settlement. Thus by the end of 1844 he had completed his organization. With a recruiting operation running smoothly in Europe and a receiving operation running smoothly in Texas, he stood ready to expand his efforts.

Expansion of the operation meant that Castro must return to Europe. He felt he could afford to do this by leaving the actual colony operation in the capable hands of Louis Huth with a base of operations firmly established. So with six months well spent in founding Castroville as the operational base, the empresario prepared to leave his colony.

CHAPTER IV

The Reorganization

By late November of 1844 Castro had established his colony in Texas substantially enough to leave the work there in the trusted hands of Louis Huth. For Castro there remained some political details in Texas to take care of and a return to Europe, where the recruiting program was experiencing difficulties. During his absence lawsuits had been filed at both Colmar and Strasbourg in France to stop Castro agents from recruiting colonists. These suits prevented recruitment of Texas colonists from those areas, and publicity concerning the suits was slowing recruitment in other areas.[1]

Thus, on November 22, 1844, the empresario left his newly formed town amid the thunderous roar of a three-salvo salute from the little cannon designed to protect the settlement from Indian attack. Before leaving, however, he delivered a rousing speech in which he reminded the colonists who was responsible for their newly acquired lands and the tremendous prosperity inevitable in their new situation. Once again his oratory served him in good stead: in one stroke he put the colonists in a good humor with a celebration and

---

[1] Legal Authorization for Louis Huth signed by Henri Castro, August 15, 1845, Ferdinand Louis Huth, Papers, Barker Texas History Center, University of Texas at Austin; Castro to Anson Jones, October 28, 1844, Colonization Papers, Archives, Texas State Library, Austin; Ashbel Smith to Anson Jones, August 13, 1844, Letters Received, Letterbook of Secretary of State Papers, Texas, Department of State Copybooks of Diplomatic Correspondence, 1836–46, Archives, Texas State Library, Austin.

gave them hope that more immigrants would soon be arriving in droves.[2]

Instructions given to Huth and others before Castro's
departure were extensive and detailed. Huth and Castro
signed an agreement leaving Huth in charge of the Texas operation during Castro's absence. The German was to be compensated with four lots of forty acres each on the McMullen
land, a thirty-by-sixteen-foot house with a shingled roof, a
5 percent commission either in money or land on the number
of colonists settled, and free provisions. Huth was promised
possession of the land in three years providing he did not re-
sign before that time. Castro also made provision for Huth to
be absent in Galveston for periods of four to six weeks on
personal business involving the shipment of goods as stipulated in their agreement signed the previous year. During the
times Huth had to be gone, Castro designated Jules Bourgeois
to be in charge of the operation on the concession. Huth could
also return to Europe providing he gave Castro six months
notice before leaving.[3]

In addition to the formal written agreement between
Huth and Castro, the empresario left detailed instructions
for the operation of the colony in his absence. He arranged
for a credit of several hundred dollars for flour, bacon, and
salt with William Elliot of San Antonio and admonished Huth
to write him in Europe at least once a month and post the
letters with Elliot. Castro designed the account with Elliot to
be used only for supplying destitute settlers who were supposed to repay the cost of the goods with their labor.

Those colonists who had no oxen received permission to
use Castro's nine pair as well as his two carts. Castro also designated several plows and other tools expected to arrive soon
at Galveston for the use of the settlers in as equitable manner
as could be devised. As new settlers arrived, they were to get
out lots of forty acres each for married men and twenty acres
for bachelors. To settle any unmanageable disputes, Castro

[2] Henri Castro, Journal, Henri Castro Papers, Barker Texas History Center,
University of Texas at Austin, 136–37.
[3] Agreement between Henri Castro and Louis Huth, November 20, 1844,
Huth Papers.

advised Huth to put the matter to a vote of the majority of the colonists.

Castro picked fifty-nine-year-old Jules Bourgeois as second in command during his absence to take Huth's place in the event of death or disability. Bourgeois could use Castro's house and garden, received free provisions, and was supplied with a pair of oxen and a cart as well as the use of a Mexican saddle horse. In return Bourgeois was charged with directing the cultivation of tobacco, sugar cane, cotton, wheat, corn, sweet potatoes, and Irish potatoes on the empresario's property. Meanwhile Castro ordered the construction of a house for both Bourgeois and Gentilz.

Finally, the empresario urged the colonists to build a church in his absence. He suggested that it be a structure sixty by thirty feet as outlined by Bishop Odin and that it be made of stone. The work on the church should be done with volunteer colonist labor. Castro left Huth to organize the settlers in any way he could to get the church built, but insisted that this work be given priority.[4]

With the colony well on its way to self-sufficiency Castro believed he had time to lobby the Texas legislature for more favorable terms on his contract. Upon leaving Castroville he traveled to Washington-on-the-Brazos and worked for prolongation of the contract. After a long legislative debate he received a two-year extension on the contract, with the stipulation that each colonist brought to the country take an oath of allegiance to the Republic of Texas prior to being permitted to settle on colony land.[5]

Castro was elated by the two-year extension. He wrote Huth that the additional time combined with the inevitable annexation of Texas to the United States was worth $500,000 to his enterprise. Furthermore, he advised the younger man to remain on the colony where his fortune was assured

[4]Unsigned Instructions, November 14, 1844, Castro to Louis Huth, July 1, 1845, Huth Papers.

[5]Castro to Anson Jones, October 11, October 28, 1844, Colonization Papers; H. P. N. Gammel, *The Laws of Texas, 1822–1897*, II: 1078; G. W. Terrell to Daingerfield, March 22, 1845, in George P. Garrison, ed., *Diplomatic Correspondence of the Republic of Texas*, I: 1184.

rather than travel to the coast to work out business difficulties with the E. Martin and Cobb Company in Galveston,
which handled the mercantile business established by Huth
and Company and Castro. The empresario spoke with the
Galveston merchants, who promised more cooperation. Then
Castro convinced Huth to remain on colony land where his
services were needed to handle the incoming colonists. He
urged Huth not to be afraid to stretch both his and Castro's
credit to the last dollar to assure the success of the colony. To
increase the security of the colony he also advised Huth to
establish a militia company at Castroville.[6]

    To bolster the number of colonists at Castroville, Castro
began to advertise in Texas newspapers. The announcement
that appeared in the Austin *Texas National Register* and the
Houston *Telegraph and Texas Register* from December 1844
until June 19, 1845 declared:

The emigrants brought to this country by Henri Castro are hereby
notified, that a settlement has been formed on the west bank of the
Medina River, twenty-five miles west of San Antonio, and that in
addition to the land secured to them by their contract, they will be
entitled to a town lot in the above settlement of Castroville. They
are further notified that if they do not claim their lands within four
months from this date, their contract will be null and void.

Any other persons desirous of settling in this desirable section of
the country, are invited to convince themselves by personal inspection, of the advantages of the site chosen for the town of Castroville, where a population of nearly two hundred souls is already
settled and forty houses erected since the third of September. They
are offered a town lot for building with a farm lot of forty acres on
the east bank of the river, on condition that they will build a house
or hut and place under cultivation fifteen acres of land in the
course of three years, when their final titles will be delivered to them.
Building materials of every description, and of the best quality, are
to be found in great abundance on the spot, and timber of all kinds
is abundant. In addition to the Medina River, numerous and permanent springs furnish a constant supply of purist water.

The most unfounded and absurd reports having been circulated
in regard to this colony by persons unfriendly to it, those who are

    [6] Castro to Louis Huth, January 1, February 6, February 11, February 18, July 1,
1845, Huth Papers.

in any way interested in its progress, may obtain information respecting it by application to the State Department Office where the certified plan of the town is deposited; or of John W. Smith, Senator; Colonel Cook and Captain Ogden, Representatives for Bexar County; Major G. T. Howard, Sheriff Bexar City; or to the authorities of Bexar County, San Antonio.

Henry [*sic*] Castro[7]

In addition to getting his hesitant colonists in Texas on the concession, Castro sought others. While in Galveston he wrote Huth that a number of Prince Carl's colonists were camped on the Lavaca River. They expressed dissatisfaction with their lot and seemed ready to disband. Castro felt that with a little encouragement they could be persuaded to go to the Castro concession. He urged Huth to encourage this tendency as much as possible.

Before he left Galveston for Europe, Castro met a shipload of his colonists led by Father Gregoire Pfanner. Castro divided this contingent of 305 people into two groups and sent them to Castroville via Port Lavaca under the leadership of Father Pfanner, who had recruited them in Alsace. Huth received instructions to have them installed under the big shed at Castroville and to make them plant corn before allowing them to begin building homes so that they would have the necessary food to survive their initial year. Bishop Odin designated Father Pfanner to act as the first priest of the colony.[8]

Traveling on to New Orleans, Castro devised a prospectus designed to recruit the American citizens he expected to flock to the colony once the republic was annexed by the United States. In this document he described the colony location as one of the best in Texas, already inhabited by 500 persons from Europe and other parts of Texas. He assured the prospective colonists that excellent transport had been arranged from the coast to the colony at reasonable cost. Once

---

[7] Austin *National Register*, December 1844–June 19, 1845; Houston *Telegraph and Texas Register*, December 1844.

[8] Castro to Louis Huth, February 6, February 11, February 18, 1845, Huth Papers.

the colonists were on the land a wooden house with a thatched roof could be built with only six weeks of work and an outlay of twenty dollars. Everything considered, he made the prospect of settling on the concession seem a reasonable and pleasant prospect. To attract U.S. citizens, he established recruiting agencies as he traveled across the country. Those contacted included James Crawford at Mobile, Alabama; Samuel Hart at Charleston, South Carolina; W. Robertson at Philadelphia, Pennsylvania; W. W. Price at New York City; and M. F. Cunningham at Boston.[9]

Later, Castro made arrangements with the Texas government to increase the number of colonists allowed on the concession from 600 to 1,000 as stipulated in his contract, for the ever-optimistic Castro anticipated a flood of new colonists. This decision in large part resulted from the action of the U.S. Congress, which moved to annex Texas in early March of 1845. Castro became so excited by the news that he wrote Huth to expect at least 4,000 colonists on the land at a very early date.[10]

Meanwhile, the empresario continued to send instructions to the ailing and overworked Huth. He urged the earliest possible settlement at Quihi Lake and ordered the hapless Huth to take possession of the other tract along the Rio Grande. Quihi presented only a minor problem, but evidently Castro had no conception of the impossibility of beginning a settlement along the Rio Grande where the proximity of Mexico kept the republic from exerting any official control. In addition he ordered that his house and garden be completed without delay, insisted that the colonists write often to Europe, and told Huth to send his reports as often as possible. In general, the empresario expressed concern that the colony be prepared to receive an influx of settlers and wanted to be apprised of every move that transpired on concession lands.[11]

[9] Castro to Louis Huth, February 11, April 13, 1845, Huth Papers; Prospectus on Texas Colonization, H. E. Haass Papers, Texas Collection, Baylor University, Waco.

[10] Castro to Ashbel Smith, March 20, 1845, Colonization Papers; Castro to Louis Huth, March 2, 1845, Huth Papers.

[11] Castro to Louis Huth, February 18, April 1, 1845, Huth Papers.

Castro arrived back in Europe in early May of 1845, where his first order of business was getting his legal problems settled so he could return to Texas as soon as possible. The legal situation originated with the accusations made against the empresario by the French chargé d'affaires in Texas, Jules de Cramayel. With this information as a basis, individuals in France filed a lawsuit against Castro, first at Strasbourg and later at Colmar. The suit stated that Castro induced colonists to go to Texas when there was in fact no land available to them because of the exposed condition of the western grants. The suit went on to charge that Castro had collected 210 francs ($42) from each colonist of which 160 francs ($32) paid for passage to Galveston and 50 francs ($10) served as a deposit Castro never intended to return. This suit had been filed in July of 1844 when Castro was absent from France and he had been found guilty in absentia for conducting a fraudulent operation.[12]

Upon arrival in France, armed with the numerous documents collected in Texas attesting to the success of his colonization project, Castro filed a countersuit. The legal maneuvers dragged on most of the summer, but by early August the court reversed its original decision against the empresario. Although Castro was vindicated, Ludwig Huth estimated that without the legal interruption there already would have been more than 1,000 landholders on the concession. Immediately on winning the case, Castro placed advertisements in all the French regional newspapers, trying to regain some of the prestige the case had cost him. Evidently this had some effect, because within two weeks of the announcements Huth and Company had sixteen new prospects clamoring to go to Texas.[13]

With the trial out of the way, a much-heartened Castro once again devoted his full energies to recruiting and settling colonists on his concession. First, he formally reorganized

[12]Castro to Louis Huth, July 1, 1845, Ludwig Huth to Louis Huth, February 28, 1845, Huth Papers; Ashbel Smith to Anson Jones, August 13, 1845, Letterbook, Secretary of State Papers, Letters Received, 521–22.

[13]Castro to Louis Huth, February 18, August 15, 1845, Ludwig Huth to Louis Huth, August 31, 1845, Huth Papers.

the operation in Texas. Louis Huth officially became director of the colony during Castro's absence and subdirector when the empresario was present at a salary of 1,500 francs ($300) annually. Castro placed Dr. George Cupples in charge of transportation from the Texas coast to the colony at an annual salary of 1,000 francs ($200). Jules Bourgeois accepted charge of cultivation for the colony, also at a salary of 1,000 francs per year. Theodore Gentilz received the title of geographical engineer and designer with the responsibility of helping the land surveyor in the distribution of lots at a salary of 500 francs ($100) per annum. All of these positions were to be paid on a semi-annual basis beginning October 1, 1845, by a commissioner in Galveston.

Castro ordered the four Texas officials to establish themselves a the colony council, which was augmented by a fifth person, the priest assigned to the Castroville church. The director, Huth, was to be president of the council, presiding at all meetings. He was to send monthly reports to Antwerp outlining in detail the progress of the colony as well as making recommendations for further colonial action. Activities of the colony were to be planned and coordinated by the council acting in concert.

Louis Huth won commendation for his work in trying to settle Quihi, but Castro urged him to push on quickly and form other towns because increasing numbers of immigrants would soon force the situation to become critical. Huth also received instructions to make advances to Cupples, Bourgeois, and Gentilz out of the first available funds. Further, Castro assured Huth that ample provisions, especially flour and salt, were being sent on each vessel leaving for Texas so that there would be no lack of food for the colonists.[14]

Meanwhile, Castro made changes in the European operation to coordinate better with Texas. An agent of the De Cocke and Bischop Company of Antwerp was hired to go to Galveston where he was to act as colony commissioner. He was responsible for paying the Texas salaries, coordinating

[14]Castro to Louis Huth, August 15, 1845, Ludwig Huth to Louis Huth, August 31, Huth Papers.

convoys to the concession, and operating the now-defunct mercantile company. At the last minute the man could not go and Castro replaced him with Albert Huth, younger brother of Louis. This new arrangement coincided with changing the point of arrival in Texas from Galveston to Corpus Christi. Cupples, acting in his capacity as transportation coordinator, received orders to dovetail his activities with the Galveston commissioner and Col. Henry Kinney at Corpus Christi, with whom Castro had made a contract to transport colonists to the concession.[15]

The need to send the business commissioner arose after the original business arrangement with the Huths developed problems. Because Louis became so tied up with his colonization efforts, the mercantile business was turned over to the E. Martin and Cobb Company of Galveston. This firm never shipped any goods back to Europe although it received a considerable amount of trade items from Huth and Company. Castro thought that he had the matter straightened out when he left Texas in February, but by July it became evident that E. Martin and Cobb was misappropriating funds and, indeed, the firm even renounced having any connection whatsoever with the colonization effort.[16]

Other changes in the European operation coincided with those in Texas. Castro appointed Huth and Company in full charge of recruiting in Baden, Alsace, and Switzerland with orders to deal with banks in the region in order to finance the enterprise. Ludwig protested that he already had more invested than he could afford and, because it seemed that some time would pass before he would get the money returned, he could not assume additional financial responsibility. He pointed out that the commission he was paying to agents, which amounted to twenty francs for family heads and ten francs for bachelors, was exceeded by advances he was forced to pay the agents. Thus the expense was too great. Castro bowed to this argument and persuaded the firm of De

[15] Castro to Louis Huth, July 1, August 15, 1845, Ludwig Huth to Louis Huth, August 31, 1845, Huth Papers.

[16] Castro to Louis Huth, February 6, July 1, 1845, Ludwig Huth to Louis Huth, February 28, August 31, 1845, Huth Papers.

Cocke and Bischop, which was acting as shipping agent in Antwerp, to assume the financial responsibility while Huth and Company continued to handle recruiting.

De Cocke and Bischop immediately inaugurated a new method of payment for the expenses of traveling to Texas. The firm charged the colonists a set fee from the place of origin to the concession property. The fee varied according to the ages of the children and the amount of baggage included, although there was a set price for adult passage. The cost of transportation, which included two hundred pounds of baggage per person as well as provisions, averaged around 600 francs ($120) per person, but could run considerably higher depending upon the amount of baggage included. De Cocke and Bischop felt that this amount would adequately cover all expenses, although the elder Huth, with his past experience in the business, seriously doubted it.[17]

At the beginning of the project in 1842 Castro had been certain that he could handle the finances of colonization, but expenses proved to be much more than he anticipated. Huth and Company, which had been conducting most of the recruiting, found finances increasingly difficult to manage. During his absence in Texas, Castro left much of the decision making in Paris to his daughter, a Mrs. Causici, whom the blunt, businesslike Ludwig Huth found very difficult to deal with. Further, merchants were increasingly reluctant to accept drafts on Castro, and the Huth organization ultimately had to assume a debt of over 5,000 francs ($1,000) on one colonist ship to keep the operation running. At one point, just before winning the court case, Castro himself considered giving up the entire project because of money worries.[18]

To make matters worse, a few disgruntled colonists straggled back to Europe and created a decidedly unfavorable public opinion against the whole enterprise. An instance of this occurred in a small town near Strasbourg, where twenty-four persons had agreed to go to Texas as soon as the weather

[17] Ludwig Huth to Louis Huth, February 28, August 31, 1845, Huth Papers.
[18] Ludwig Huth to Louis Huth, November 28, December 18, 1844, and February 28, March 5, August 15, August 31, 1845, Huth Papers.

permitted. During February of 1845 a woman named Weber with two small children returned to that village after spending some time in Texas as colonists. She related a horrible story of suffering in which her husband died of starvation between Victoria and San Antonio while others succumbed to fevers and disease. She pointed out that in addition to disease and lack of food there were other, perhaps more horrible, fates, such as that which befell young Ziliac Rhin of her caravan, who was murdered by Indians. She strongly advised any with whom she talked against going to Texas. Her story caused all but four of the twenty-four prospective colonists to cancel their contracts. Naturally, colorful stories of this nature from individuals well known in their native villages had a decidedly adverse effect on recruiting and frequently spread.[19]

The unfortunate experiences of many of the colonists prompted departmental prefects to send circulars to the mayors of the various towns advising them to do everything in their power to discourage citizens from emigrating to Texas. Despite such opposition, the ever-optimistic Castro was confident he could counteract this adverse situation as he had similar ones in the past with newspaper advertising and help from influential people friendly to him.[20]

Perhaps this situation caused the empresario to try to develop new areas for recruiting. Earlier he had experienced some success with Swiss colonists, so he began to increase recruiting activities in Switzerland. Almost immediately he had a tremendous response. A large number of Swiss Catholics expressed interest in going to Texas. He estimated that approximately 17,000 were eager to leave their country because of religious persecution. As Castro explained to Bishop Odin, who happened to be in France seeking financial aid for the church in Texas, these emigrants would begin leaving Antwerp for Texas in August in twenty to thirty ships, de-

---

[19] Ludwig Huth to Louis Huth, February 28, 1845, Huth Papers.

[20] August Huth to Louis Huth, April 14, 1845, Ludwig Huth to Louis Huth, August 31, 1845, Huth Papers; Castro to Ashbel Smith, December 25, 1843, Colonization Papers.

parting every six days until April of 1846.[21] Evidently the
great Swiss migration was only a hopeful expectation on Castro's part, because no mention is made of it beyond the state-
ments to Bishop Odin. Several Swiss families became colonists, but not in numbers that compare with the empresario's
hopes.

Thus during the summer of 1845, as Castro solved his
legal problems and began to have more success in recruiting,
finance assumed overriding importance. Ludwig Huth had
been concerned for sometime about the shaky financial situation of the operation, and had indicated to Castro that he
should seek additional financing. Apparently the empresario
also began to have serious doubts about his continued ability
to underwrite the project alone because he began looking for
large-scale monetary assistance that summer. By August he
had located a group of businessmen in Antwerp who were
willing to invest in the operation.[22]

With the able assistance of Ludwig Huth, Castro consummated the deal on November 19, 1845. They formed a
corporation that put the entire concession under the ownership of the Société de Colonisation Europée-Américain au
Texas with headquarters in Antwerp, and with Guillaume
Dhanis, the head of a large Antwerp banking firm, at its head.
Thus the entire complexion of the operation changed as Castro lost the absolute control he had exercised up until this
point.

The empresario paid dearly for the necessary aid to continue his colonization project. The company was capitalized
at 500,000 francs ($100,000) with Castro receiving a six-
twentieth interest for the 150,000 francs ($30,000) he already
had invested in the operation. Eleven investors, including
Huth and Company, divided the other 350,000 francs. The
eleven had to put up only 87,500 francs, which was considered enough to run the company for its stated lifetime of five
years. The corporation forced Castro to put under company

[21] Odin to Society for the Propagation of the Faith, May 23, 1845, Odin to
Blanc, May 30, 1845, Odin to Timon, May 30, August 1, 1845, Odin Papers, Catholic Archives of Texas, Austin.

[22] Ludwig Huth to Louis Huth, February 28, August 31, 1845, Huth Papers.

control all the 269 concession contracts he had written in the previous three years as well as the remaining vacant lots in Castroville and any other lands he owned in Texas. He retained only one exception, a deed for a league of land (4,400 acres) that he pledged as security.

Dhanis, as manager, plus two directors were required to give permission before any major activities took place. Those three retained complete control over the project including full authority in recruiting colonists and getting them to the concession, in all financial matters, and in taking possession of and disposing of concession lands. Castro became general manager in Texas, operating in much the same manner as before, except he had to give a monthly report on all matters pertaining to the project to Dhanis.

The profits expected from the operation were to be divided among the twelve investors. The first 500,000 francs were to reimburse their investment plus interest of 5 percent per annum. After they regained the initial investment, the remaining profits were to be divided with one-half going to Castro and the other half divided among the other investors. Castro could not sell his six-twentieth share in the company for any reason.[23]

Immediately upon formation, the corporation informed the Texas government and Louis Huth of the change. Huth received assurance that he would remain in his position in Texas, which was indispensable to the successful completion of the enterprise. Additionally, the company urged him once again to start the colony on the concession property bordering the Rio Grande River. Castro and his new partners sought to expand their operation as rapidly as possible.[24]

With the act of taking partners in the enterprise, Castro relegated his own role in the operation to that of agent for the company. Nevertheless, it seemed a necessary step be-

[23] Agreement forming the Société de Colonisation Europée-Américain au Texas, November 19, 1845, Colonization Papers; this same agreement appears in the Deed Records, Bexar County Clerk's Office, Bexar County Courthouse, San Antonio, Book FI, 283–88.

[24] Castro to Anson Jones, December 1, 1845, Castro to Ashbel Smith, December 1, 1845, Colonization Papers; Castro to Louis Huth, December 1, 1845, G. Dhanis to Louis Huth, December 1, 1845, Huth Papers.

cause the operation was getting too large and expensive for one man alone. If things worked out as anticipated, then there was still a fortune to be made from the enterprise, even if the empresario's share was only 50 percent of the expected profits.

The reorganized company inherited an experienced recruiting operation. From the time Castro began to recruit colonists an efficient method of processing personnel for their journey to concession property gradually had been devised. During the preceding three years of activity the system had been refined and revised until by late 1845 it represented a sound practical operation.

Several recruiting techniques tended to become standardized. Recruiters tried to get groups to emigrate, rather than individuals. With this in mind the empresario particularly wanted as many clergymen as possible to make the voyage so that their immense influence would convince large segments of their European congregations to follow them. As early as the sailing of the *Louis Philippe* in January of 1843, Castro had ministers in the colonial complement. At that time Father Menetrier Aumont made the trip in order to report back to his parishioners in France on the feasibility of emigrating to Texas in large numbers.[25]

There are numerous examples of getting churchmen to increase immigration, but perhaps the most successful effort involved Father Gregoire Pfanner and part of his congregation. Father Pfanner spoke with Huth and Company about the possibility of leading a large group of Haut Rhin citizens to the colony in mid-1844. Ultimately he and his contingent of three hundred colonists sailed on the vessel *Probus*, arriving at Galveston in February of 1845, just before Castro returned to Europe. Although their presence greatly swelled the numbers of colonists on the grant, they caused considerable damage to the project when Father Pfanner became disillusioned with the whole scheme and wrote extensively to newspapers in Alsace denouncing the colonization project.[26]

[25] Société de Colonisation Europée-Américain au Texas, Menke Collection; Castro to Anson Jones, February 20, 1843, Colonization Papers.
[26] Castro to Louis Huth, February 6, 1845, Ludwig Huth to Louis Huth, February 28, August 31, 1845, *Courrier d'Alsace*, August 27, 1846, Huth Papers.

Another example of group recruiting was the case of a Mr. Riegert from Leingolsheim near Strasbourg, who made a deal with Castro to transport a group of twenty-five Alsatian farmers to the colony at his own expense. In return the farmers were required to work for Riegert for a ten-year period to repay him for the transportation costs. As compensation Castro agreed to give the man 1,000 acres of concession land for his recruiting services. This very lucrative deal apparently was never consummated, but it is indicative of the type of recruiting activities that went on in Europe.[27]

To attract colonists other than by personal contact, the company used rather sophisticated advertising, both in newspapers and extensively through pamphlets. In the pamphlets the empresario went to great lengths to illustrate Texas as a bountiful land whose fertile soil awaited only the diligent efforts of a hard-working European class of farmer to make it bloom forth. It is ironic that large passages, indeed even whole sections, of these pamphlets were lifted verbatim from the publication for the French Ministry of Agriculture produced by Castro's old enemy, Bourgeois d'Orvanne. Wherever he got his information, the empresario distributed the pamphlets throughout recruiting areas and printed many of them bilingually with French on one page and German on the facing page.[28]

For Henri Castro, financial considerations dominated the year 1845. Money problems, legal hassles, and a myriad of details tested to the utmost his seemingly endless supply of energy. Yet, the ever-optimistic empresario remained convinced that a fantastic fortune awaited him in the El Dorado of Texas land. Thousands of prospective colonists beckoned just out of his grasp both in the United States as well as Eu-

[27] Ludwig Huth to Louis Huth, March 21, 1844, Castro to Louis Huth, December 1, 1843, Huth Papers.

[28] *Courrier d'Alsace*, October 1, 1846, Huth Papers; Lorenzo Castro, *Immigration from Alsace-Lorraine, A Brief Sketch of Henry Castro's Colony in Western Texas*, II; Henri Castro, "Le Texas Appercu Historique et Statistique," Henri Castro Papers, Barker Texas History Center, The University of Texas at Austin; Henri Castro, "Le Texas," H. E. Haass Papers, Texas Collection, Baylor University; France, Ministere de l'Agriculture et du Commerce, Documens su le Commerce Exterieur, Texas, in Thomas W. Streeter, *Bibliography of Texas*, III: 415; Henri Castro, "Le Texas," in Streeter, *Bibliography*, III: 409.

rope, where the prospect of massive Swiss emigration became so alluring.

Evidently he had little trouble selling his dream to the calculating businessmen of Antwerp. His boundless enthusiasm for Texas land seemed to overcome all obstacles. There is little doubt that, like all gamblers, he was confident that, with only a bit more money to finance him, the bonanza would materialize. Thus he sold his concession and prepared to work with a will to bring his dream to fruition.

CHAPTER V

Settling the Grant, 1845–47

W HEN Castro left Texas in February of 1845, he left Louis
Huth in complete control of the colonization program there.
The empresario expected Huth to settle the colonists on
their property quickly and even expand the operation to the
Rio Grande concessions. This optimistic expectation was not
so easily realized. Numerous problems and delays prevented
the rapid settlement of the colony. Those problems already
had begun to develop in April of 1845 when the charismatic
Castro boarded ship for Europe.[1]

The week Castro took leave of Texas in February of
1845 more than 300 colonists arrived at Galveston under the
leadership of the priest, Gregoire Pfanner. Huth, who made
the arrangements for the transport and care of the new colonists, moved them to Castroville without unusual incident in
the usual time of approximately one month. At that point
considerable difficulty arose because of a conflict in leadership perceptions between Pfanner and colony officials. This
confrontation threw the operation into a state of confusion
and played a major role in delaying settlement of the grant
for a year.[2]

Of the 309 passengers on the *Probus* and *Norvegian*, the

[1]Agreement Between Henri Castro and Louis Huth, November 20, 1844,
Legal Authorization signed by Henri Castro, August 15, 1845, Castro to Louis
Huth, February 18, April 1, 1845, Ferdinand Louis Huth Papers, Barker Texas His-
tory Center, University of Texas at Austin.
[2]Castro to Louis Huth, February 6, February 11, February 18, 1845, Huth
Papers.

vessels that brought Pfanner's group, 113 were heads of
households eligible to receive grants. The *Probus* carried
Pfanner and another priest named Lienhard, while the *Norvegian* contingent was led by yet another priest, Father Jean
Roesch. The overwhelming majority of this entire group of
immigrants came from Haut Rhin, where Pfanner had a
church. Most of them were farmers. None of the members of
this group declared any property, because most of them were
actually destitute; they depended entirely on the colonization organization for help in getting settled.[3]

Pfanner had recruited most of these people personally
from his parish in Haut Rhin and felt a strong responsibility
toward them. The priest received his first unfavorable impression of Texas as he passed through the fever-ridden
coastal plain from Lavaca Bay to Castroville where several of
his followers fell victim to the coastal fevers. Upon arrival at
the new town, he was aghast to find that Huth, whom Castro
had assured him would place him and his people in possession of their property, was only a simple merchant. To one
newly arrived from Europe, where status meant a great deal,
this seemed a totally unacceptable situation.[4]

The wary priest refused to allow Huth any control over
his people until he personally inspected all aspects of the situation. Pfanner traveled to Austin and other parts of Texas
where he viewed much better agricultural properties than
those of the concession. However, those lands proved expensive, and his followers, who were in poor financial circumstance when they left Europe, now depended totally upon
colony officials in Texas for their financial well-being. This
made it impossible for them to leave and buy the better lands
or even to return to their homeland. Further, the priest la-
mented the high cost of food. He did concede that cattle raising offered a major possibility for profit, although the lack of
an immediate market deferred those profits to a later date.
He echoed the warnings of the Texas government and most

[3]Ships' Lists for *Probus and Norvegian*, Colonization Papers, Archives, Texas
State Library, Austin.
[4]Ludwig Huth to Louis Huth, March 5, 1845, Castro to Louis Huth, February
18, 1845, *Courrier d'Alsace*, August 27, 1846, Huth Papers.

others involved in bringing immigrants to Texas when he said that potential settlers from Europe should bring enough money with them to maintain themselves for at least a year. His belated awareness of this necessity did little to help his followers' sad situation.[5]

General considerations aside, the priest's primary quarrel with colony officials concerned property due the colonists according to their contracts. Castro intended to establish a series of towns encircling the grant. Each village would be laid out in town lots with outlying twenty- and forty-acre plots available to the colonists, in a pattern similar to that at Castroville. This would allow the settlers to congregate in the familiar European village life-style while farming the small nearby fields. It also offered them group protection against possible Indian attack. Later the colonists could take possession of their actual granted properties that lay in the immediate vicinity. Thus as the grant became ringed with European-style villages, the interior would contain all the large granted properties.[6]

Pfanner disagreed with this concept because of the way it was implemented. Since he suspected that the twenty- and forty-acre plots represented all the land the colonists were going to receive despite the terms of their contracts, he demanded that the colonists be allowed to choose any of the 320- or 640-acre plots of land they wanted as long as the plots lay within the confines of the grant. This differed from the way Castro and Huth envisioned the process. They reserved the right to establish the villages in an orderly manner with colonists drawing lots for their large acreages that would be in close proximity to their particular village. Meanwhile, Pfanner inspected the grant and located for his people what he felt was the best available property on the Frio River some distance from Castroville. Huth refused to allow settlement there and insisted that the people settle on Quihi Lake. This location, much closer to Castroville, would be safer and also had abundant food and water. Pfanner refused to allow his

[5] *Courrier d'Alsace*, August 27, 1846, Huth Papers.
[6] *Courrier d'Alsace*, October 1, 1846, Huth Papers.

people to settle at Quihi and the ensuing empasse dragged on all year while Castro was tied up settling legal problems in Europe.[7]

Although the Pfanner episode created considerable difficulty for the colony, the priest remains a shadowy figure. He may have been motivated in part by the desire to collect a commission of 25 acres per family for people he introduced into the colony. Evidently protecting his potential profits of 3,145 acres acquired overriding significance because there is no record of any outstanding church work done by him other than four baptisms recorded in the parish register at Castroville. Indeed, grand juries in San Antonio and Victoria apparently indicted him for fraud and murder, although neither case came to trial. His actions caused Father John Brands, who supervised Texas church activities during the temporary absence of Bishop Odin, to take action against Pfanner in June of 1845. At that time he stated: "I have been obliged to interdict the priest at Castroville, whose scandalous conduct has not only deserved all the local censure but even the penitentiary; he had set the whole colony of Castro in confusion." Pfanner remained in the area for a time, but by August of 1846 he had left Texas for Mexico.[8]

Early in 1846 the *Alberdina* arrived in Texas with eighty-eight colonists constituting twenty-nine families. Huth quickly persuaded ten of the newly arrived families to settle at Quihi. This activity encouraged fourteen of the families waiting at Castroville to join in the enterprise although only one of the Pfanner contingent, Ambrose Reitzer, joined. This little group of pioneers led by Louis Huth; surveyor, Charles De-Montel; engineer and draftsman, Theodore Gentilz; and Castroville's constable, G. L. Haass, left in early March of

[7] *Courrier d'Alsace*, September 4, 1846, Huth Papers.

[8] Ludwig Huth to Louis Huth, March 5, 1845, *Courrier d'Alsace*, August 27, 1846, Huth Papers; Parish Register, St. Louis Catholic Church, Castroville, Texas, I: 4no.36, 12no.114, 14no.141, 14no.182; Jean Marie Odin, Journal, 1842–43, typescript, Diocesan Records, Diocese of Galveston-Houston, Houston, entries in the spring of 1845; Sister Mary Generosa Callahan, C.D.P., *History of the Sisters of Divine Providence*, 71–72; Theodore D. Gittenger, "A History of St. Louis Catholic Church of Castroville, Texas" (Master's thesis, Sam Houston State University, 1972), 12–16.

1846 to establish the first settlement within the bounds of Castro's concession. The caravan of carts traveled the ten miles from Castroville to Quihi Lake in one day without incident and the group camped that night on the banks of Quihi Lake with every expectation of a totally successful future.[9]

The next day Huth distributed the twenty- and forty-acre plots to the respective single and married men and admonished the settlers to build their homes and prepare the ground for spring planting. He and the other colony officials returned to Castroville, leaving James Brown and David Burnham, both experienced frontiersmen, to provide the colonists with game that abounded in the area. Brown and Burnham were also designated to supervise the colonists in establishing their new homes while Augustin Trevino was hired to serve as teamster and cattle-raising instructor. Huth also provided the colonists with bacon and corn meal, along with plenty of tools to assist them in clearing the land and building their houses.[10]

Bustling activity permeated the settlement as the newly arrived settlers began building temporary homes and preparing the ground for planting. Then disaster struck the fledgling community. About a week after they arrived, the Brinkhoff family, consisting of Henry, his wife Gertrude, their three small boys as well as Henry's father and sister camped about a mile downstream from the lake. Late one night a shot rang out and a bullet pierced their tent wall, striking one of the children. The women, thinking that the shot was fired by a neighbor hunting turkeys, rushed to the door shouting a warning to stop firing. Instead, they faced a party of Lipan Apache Indians who killed five members of the family and abducted two small boys. This affair had a

[9] Undated account and list of first settlers at Quihi, Huth Papers; Ships' Lists for the *Probus, Norvegian,* and *Alberdina,* Colonization Papers. The traditional accounts of the settlement of Quihi credit ten families with starting the settlement, but checking the account written by Louis Huth against the ships' lists indicates that the group totaled twenty-four families, ten of which had just arrived on the *Alberdina.*

[10] Rudolph Schoroning to Lorenzo Castro, September, 1879, *San Antonio Texas Sun,* March, 1880; Josie M. Rothe, "Quihi, Born Amidst the Turbulence of Old Times, is at Peace Today," *San Antonio Light,* January 13, 1935; W. N. Saathoff, "Quihi, Settled 105 Years Ago," Hondo *Anvil Herald,* July 22, 1949.

chilling effect on all the colonists, causing several of the Quihi families to move immediately to San Antonio rather than risk the danger of an exposed frontier life.[11]

It happened that Quihi Lake provided a convenient camping spot on a well-traveled north-south Indian trail, which made the location well known to various tribes. This, however, did not deter the settlers who remained at the village. They built a semicircular brush enclosure on the banks of the lake where many of them slept during periods of danger from Indian attack. These immigrants, only days in Texas, were entirely unprepared for this type of experience. They had few firearms and had not expected emergencies like Indian raids to be a part of their new life.[12]

Meanwhile the Antwerp Society expanded the colonization operation and increased emigration. Three vessels left Europe for the colony in January of 1846 with fewer than ten colonists on each, but on March 25 the *Cronstadt* sailed from Antwerp with 102 colonists aboard. The newly organized company dispatched nine additional ships in 1846, which brought the total potential settlers arriving in Texas that year to approximately 1,000. This increased activity also resulted from a change in recruiting technique. Of the thirteen vessels leaving in 1846, five of them sailed from Bremen, carrying passengers recruited not from the Rhine area but from interior German states. Indeed, some of the Bremen sailings represented cooperative efforts of an avowed competitor of the Antwerp Society, the Adelsverein, which was settling New Braunfels, some thirty miles north of San Antonio. It became a matter of expediency that, when neither of the organizations had enough passengers to fill a particular ship, they temporarily combined forces.[13]

[11] Unsigned account of the Quihi massacre in Louis Huth's handwriting, Huth Papers; Claude Dubuis to unknown person in France, October 25, 1847, H. E. Haass Papers, Texas Collection, Baylor University; Ship's List for the *Alberdina*, Colonization Papers.

[12] Map of Castro's Colony, ca. 1856, General Land Office of Texas, Files of Original Land Owners, Austin; Rudolph Schorobing to Lorenzo Castro, September 1, 1879, *San Antonio Texas Sun*, March, 1880; Rothe, "Quihi."

[13] Guillaume Dhanis to Louis Huth, March 25, May 6, May 12, 1846, Huth Papers. These letters plus the ships' lists in the Colonization Papers indicate that the

Once again with the resumption of immigrant arrivals, Huth began to get detailed instructions on how to handle the colonists. When the first large group left Europe in March destined for Corpus Christi, both Castro and Dhanis anxiously urged that Huth make arrangements with Colonel Kinney there for sending the colonists overland to the colony. They felt it important for the enterprise that the first colonists of 1846 create a good impression on those to follow.

In May Dhanis wrote that eight ships were leaving Bremen filled with immigrants who had not signed contracts with either the Adelsverein or the Antwerp Society. He emphasized that if Castro, who had just left for Texas, arrived before them, he probably could get the entire contingent to go to the Castro colony because its members already were leaning in that direction. Once again he urged Huth to take good care of the immigrants, of whom 202 had left on the vessel *Bangor* a few days earlier. Then he scolded Huth for not answering his letter of January 1. Evidently the slow-mail problem that had so vexed Huth and Castro in the past also created communication difficulties for Dhanis and the new company.

Castro left Antwerp by steamer for Texas on May 14, 1846, the same day that his family departed as part of the 202 passengers on the sailing ship *Bangor*. He arrived at Galveston on July 3, well ahead of the sailing vessel, and began to make immediate preparations to transport 600 colonists from the coast to Castroville. A messenger from Huth met

---

ships sailing in 1846 transporting Castro colonists included the *Euphrasina* in January from Ghent with an unknown number of passengers; the *Talisman* from Antwerp on January 2 with nine passengers; the *Diamont* from Antwerp on January 21 with four passengers; the *Cronstadt* from Antwerp on March 25 with 102 passengers; the *Carl Wilhelm* from Bremen, date unknown, with an unknown number of passengers; the *Louis Frederick* from Bremen, date unknown, with 103 passengers, arriving in Texas on June 9; the *Neptune* from Bremen, date unknown, with an unknown number of passengers; the *Bangor* from Antwerp on May 14 with 202 passengers; the *Leo* from Bremen on April 15 with eighty passengers; the *Flora* from unknown port on July 7 with unknown number of passengers; the *Feyen* from Bremen on unknown date with an unknown number of passengers; the *Schanunga* from Antwerp on September 15 with 137 passengers; and the *Duc de Brabant* from Antwerp in October with 200 passengers.

him there and told Castro about several letters the empresario had never received. This prompted the empresario to
send an express courier to Huth at Castroville because he
was convinced that enemies were intercepting his, Huth's,
and the society's letters. Castro ordered Huth to make preparations to receive the new flood of settlers. The empresario
wanted the large receiving shed put in order, his stone house
prepared with Madeira and Bordeaux grape vines planted
on the lot behind the structure, and John James to be sum-
moned immediately to survey all of the 160- and 320-acre
plots before his arrival. Further, he ordered Huth to send all
available horses along with as many carts as possible to Lavaca as soon as he could get them started.[14]

Castro sent to Castroville, as planned, the colonists who
arrived at Galveston during July and August of 1846, while
he remained in Galveston. Huth managed to settle fifty of
the new families at the second settlement on the grant called
Vandenburgh on Verde Creek about five or six miles from
Quihi. This second settlement within the bounds of the grant
began on September 12 with Jules Bourgeois in charge of the
operation. It was surveyed in the same manner as Quihi with
colonists receiving twenty- and forty-acre plots to farm in addition to town lots until the actual granted property could be
distributed.[15]

Meanwhile, the flow of colonists from Europe continued. The Antwerp Society managed to keep an active recruiting program going through the work of Huth and Company at Neufreystaedt, H. and C. Cremavesi at Bremen, and
Mr. Sloman at Hamburg, in addition to the central offices of
the organization at Antwerp. Various newspapers in Europe
were supplied with information concerning the Texas colony
in order to facilitate recruiting, as well as to offset adverse
publicity generated by supporters of the Adelsverein who

[14] Guillaume Dhanis to Louis Huth, March 25, May 6, 1846, Castro to Louis Huth, July 6, 1846, Huth Papers.
[15] Castro to Bishop Odin, December 28, 1846, and January 14, 1847, Rever-end Claude Dubuis to Bishop Odin, April 29, 1847, Diocese of Galveston-Houston Archives; Ludwig Huth to Albert Huth, July 9, 1847, Huth Papers; "Leinweber Family History," Leinweber File, James Menke Collection, San Antonio.

Henri Castro at about the time of the Civil War (From *Castroville and Henry Castro*, courtesy Standard Printing Company)

The State of Texas, }
COUNTY OF MEDINA. }

No. 126

ACRES. 320

THIS IS TO CERTIFY THAT *Florian Braunek*

appeared before me, Commissioner, appointed by virtue of "an act to perfect land titles in Castro's Colony," and made oath that he was introduced into Texas previous to the 15th day of February, A. D. 1847, by H. Castro, according to a contract signed between them in virtue of the Colonization Contract of said H. Castro with the Government of Texas, and also proved the facts by two respectable witnesses; and the said *Florian Braunek* being a single man over 17 years of age, at the time of his emigration, is entitled to *Three hundred and twenty* acres of land. And the said *Florian Braunek* having designated the land assigned to him within said Colony Grant, is entitled to a Patent for the same, which land is designated on the plat and field-notes of surveys made by virtue of said Colonization Contract, as *Surveys Nos 260 & 384 in District No 1 on the waters of the Seco creek a branch of the Rio Frio*

Given under my hand and Official Seal at Castroville, this 31st Day of October A. D. 1850

J. M. Carolan Com.

Land certificate for a Castro Colony grant issued to Florian Braunek by Commissioner Carolan. (Courtesy General Land Office of Texas)

Zwischen den Unterzeichneten,

den Verein zum
Schutze der Einwanderer in Texas,

G.ᵐᵉ DHANIS & C.ⁱᵉ

errichtet in Antwerpen,

laut Acte ausgestellt vom Notar J. HANEGRAEFF

den 25 Februar 1846.

einerseits

und H.ᵇ

anderseits,

ist nachstehender Vertrag zu Stande gekommen:

Kraft eines Gesetzes der Republik von Texas, vom 15ᵗᵉⁿ Februar, Eintausend achthundert zwei und vierzig, und eines am fünfzehnten gleichen Monats zu Austin, durch den Herrn General *Samuel Houston*, Präsident der Republik, unterzeichneten Contrakts, ist Herr H. Castro, Concessionär eines bedeutenden Strich Landes in der Grafschaft Sant-Antonio von Bexar, in Texas. Derselbe beginnt am Loredo, läuft auf das linke Ufer des Rio-Frio, ferner der Länge der Strasse Loredo nach, wo sich der Rio-Frio und die Gewässer der Medina theilen, bis zum gleich entfernten Punkt der beiden Flüsse ; ferner Längs der Medina, bis zwanzig Meilen nördlich über der Strasse des Presidio-Rio-Grande; ferner in gerader Linie bis zum Zusammenfluss des Arro-ijs-de-Walde und des Río-Frio, und endlich der Länge nach des linken Ufers des Hauptarms des Rio-Frio bis zum Anfangspunkt.

Diese Concession ist Herrn Castro unter der Bedingung

Entre les soussignés,

la Société de Colonisation au Texas,

G.ᵐᵉ DHANIS & C.ⁱᵉ

établie à Anvers,

par acte passé le 25 février 1846, devant le

notaire J. HANEGRAEFF,

d'une part

et Mᵐᵉ Vᵉ *Maria Derungs.*

d'autre part,

a été conclu le traité suivant :

En vertu d'une loi de la République du Texas, passée le 15 février mil huit cent quarante deux, et d'un contrat signé à Austin le quinze du même mois par M. le général *Samuel Houston*, président de la République, M. H. Castro est concessionnaire de terres considérables dans le Comté de Saint-Antonio de Bexar, au Texas, commençant au Loredo, traversant sur la rive gauche du Rió-Frio, ensuite le long de la route Loredo au point où se divise le Rió-Frio et les eaux de la rivière Medina jusqu'au point également distant des deux rivières. Ensuite le long de la Medina jusqu'au point vingt milles nord au-dessus de la route du Présidio-Rio-Grande. Ensuite en ligne directe au point du confluent de l'Arroyo-de-Waldé et du Rió-Frio. Ensuite le long de la rive gauche de la principale branche dn Rio-Frio jusqu'au point de départ.

First page of a colonization contract between the Antwerp Company and Maria Derungs. (Courtesy Library of the Daughters of the Republic of Texas at the Alamo)

Castroville in the late 1840s, as drawn by Theodore Gentilz. (Courtesy Barker Texas History Center, University of Texas at Austin)

The Groff family of Medina County, Texas, in front of their typical Alsatian-style home. (Courtesy Castroville Public Library)

St. Louis Catholic Church, with the 1850 church in the foreground, the 1870 church immediately behind it, and the 1846 church in the background. (Courtesy Ruth Lawler, Castroville; copy from University of Texas Institute of Texan Cultures, San Antonio)

The 1870 St. Louis Catholic Church (right), with the Moye Academy to the left, about 1908. (Courtesy Bob Johnson, Castroville; copy from University of Texas Institute of Texan Cultures, San Antonio)

Left: Bishop Jean Marie Odin, who was instrumental in making Castro's colony a success in its earliest days. (Courtesy Diocese of Galveston-Houston) *Right:* Father Claude Marie Dubuis, first permanent priest at Castroville and later second Catholic bishop in Texas.

A drawing of Castroville by Theodore Gentilz, about 1850. (Courtesy Library of the Daughters of the Republic of Texas at the Alamo)

The Landmark Inn, Castroville. (Courtesy Library of the Daughters of the Republic of Texas at the Alamo)

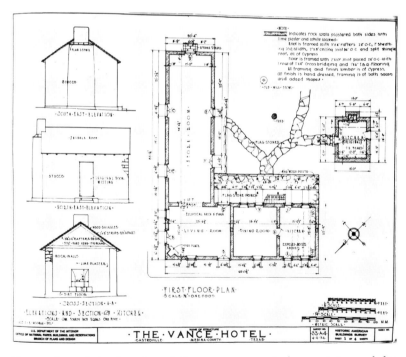

Floor plan of the Landmark Inn, now operated as a state park by the Texas Parks and Wildlife Department. (Courtesy Library of Congress)

Theodore Gentilz, who acted in several official capacities in the early days of Castro's colony, left the only visual record of that period. (Courtesy Library of the Republic of Texas at the Alamo)

delighted in spreading news of events like the massacre at Quihi. The articles produced by the Antwerp Society assured Europeans that the lands in Castro's colony were fertile, well watered, protected from danger, and above all free to European colonists. They warned, however, that those who failed to arrive in Texas prior to the end of the concession contract on February 15, 1847, would have to pay the equivalent of $1.25 per acre for lands held by the Antwerp Society.[16]

The success of the European recruiting operation began to tax Castro's resources in Texas. He began searching for alternative routes to Castroville rather than the traditional trip by sea to Lavaca Bay, then overland to San Antonio. Evidently the competition from the Adelsverein, which used the same route through its port of Carlshaven, later Indianola, on Lavaca Bay influenced this changed attitude. Additionally, the Mexican War, which began in May of 1846, greatly accelerated shipping to the Texas coast, particularly the Corpus Christi area, making vessels easier to charter for that part of Texas. Thus in November Castro signed a contract with James Powers to transport colonists and their freight from Copano Bay, only a short distance from Victoria and Corpus Christi, to Castroville at a rate of $2.50 per hundredweight. This new route from Galveston to Copano Bay and thence overland to the colony shortened the land travel, decreased drayage costs, and removed the colonists from prolonged contact with Adelsverein officials, who in the past had lured Castro colonists to their colony at New Braunfels.[17]

During the winter of 1846 Gentilz surveyed town lots and field plots for a third village to be established on Parker Creek approximately twenty-five miles west of Castroville. Early in February of 1847 the first colonists arrived on the site and by August the village was firmly established with twenty-nine families in residence. This town, named Dhanis in honor of Guillaume Dhanis who was acting as president of

[16] Antwerp *Precursor*, August 20, 1846, Fitzsimon Papers, Amarillo Public Library, Amarillo; Colmar (Germany) *Diskalia*, September 23, 1846; Colmar (Germany) *Courrier d'Alsace*, August 27, September 4, October 1, 1846, Huth Papers.

[17] Contract between H. Castro and J. Powers, November 21, 1846, Fitzsimon Papers.

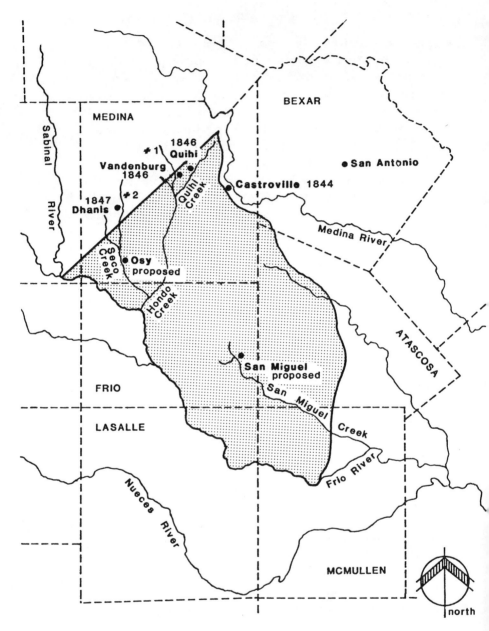

CASTRO'S COLONY: TOWNS FOUNDED

#1 Verde Creek   #2 Parker Creek

- - - - County boundaries   ▬▬▬ Grant boundary

the society, undoubtedly represented an attempt by Castro to keep the Belgian partners in a good humor. It became the westernmost settlement founded by Castro. Like the others, it stood not on granted land but on private property with lots in the village and twenty- and forty-acre subsistence plots allotted to the settlers so that they could survive until they could claim their granted lands.[18]

The founding of Dhanis coincided with the expiration of the concession contract. After February 15, 1847, Castro could import no more colonists into Texas to receive free concession land. At this point Castro and his partners planned to begin to sell the property in their possession that amounted to 50 percent of that granted to the colonists as stipulated in the individual contracts. Furthermore, they planned to sell the premium property, of ten sections (6,400 acres) for every one hundred heads of households introduced under the original contract, at a rate of $1.25 per acre to recruits from Europe. These recruits would be secured in the same manner as those already transported to Texas through the existing organization. The new colonists would differ from old ones because they would have to pay for their property rather than receive it free. The neatly packaged operation seemed certain to make all the investors wealthy, particularly when it was viewed from the security of an Antwerp business office.[19]

As computed by the society, the organization could expect no less than 64,000 acres of premium land. Further, the one-half property payment made by the colonists amounted to approximately 240,000 acres, which would give the organization slightly over 300,000 acres to sell. At $1.25 per acre this represented a total income of $375,000 on an investment of $100,000. With this kind of expected return, the Europeans were eager to invest.[20]

[18] Josie R. Finger, *125th Parish Anniversary of St. Dominic's Catholic Church at Old D'Hanis, Texas* (privately published, 1972), unnumbered pages; Castro to Bishop Odin, December 28, 1846, Catholic Archives, Diocese of Galveston-Houston.

[19] Antwerp *Precursor*, August 20, 1846, Fitzsimon Papers.

[20] Guillaume Dhanis to Ludwig Huth in letter from Ludwig Huth to Louis Huth, April 21, 1847, Huth Papers. This letter mentioned that the society expected 390,000 total acres to accrue to the organization. This was stressed as an approximation because the members were unaware of the total number of contracts signed by colonists.

In actual practice the plan had several flaws. First and most important, the colonists had no land in their possession, nor did Castro or the society have possession of any concession property. Although the empresario had surveyed part of the concession and had even issued certificates that designated the lands individual colonists would receive, the State of Texas never had conferred title on any colonist nor had it given any premium lands to Castro or the society. Further, the location of the land on the outer edge of the frontier made it virtually worthless. Only the property close to Castroville had any value and even there the best improved land was worth only one dollar per acre. Thus the investors back in Europe who were anticipating a tidy profit on their arrangement were in for a rude shock, and by the spring of 1847 they were beginning to get an inkling of what was in the offing.[21]

The financial problems of the project dated back to 1845 when Louis Huth faced the first of seemingly unending problems of inadequate financing in Texas. It began with the arrangement with William Elliott for supplies, which proved to be totally inadequate, and finally resulted in Elliott cutting off all credit. Fortunately, no vessels bringing more immigrants arrived in 1845 after Pfanner's large complement in February. But the empresario's success in Europe indicated that a deluge of colonists would arrive the following year. Huth was forced to use 3,000 francs ($600) of his own funds to keep the operation going until March of 1846, when Castro finally arranged a credit of 1,500 francs ($300) in New Orleans to tide the enterprise over.

Once Castro returned to Texas, he resumed complete charge of matters. Just prior to leaving Europe he had renegotiated his contract with the Antwerp Society. This new business relationship was much more to his liking. In the most significant change, Castro retained possession of all of the McMullen grant, which included the town of Castroville along with the town out lots of twenty and forty acres each. It

[21] Survey of land values in deed records of the Medina County Courthouse at Hondo for the years 1849–50.

also gave him possession of several other properties not included in his concession. Additionally, a stock redistribution within the company aided the empresario somewhat. Thus he seemed to be in good shape financially when he arrived in Texas.[22]

But Castro departed from Europe under circumstances less favorable than they seemed at first glance. The bankrupt empresario had left numerous creditors and at least one major lawsuit behind him. He owed Ludwig Hugh 16,000 francs ($3,200) from the original mercantile deal they made back in 1843 as well as 2,800 francs ($560) for legal fees the elder Huth paid during Castro's court fight at Strasbourg and Colmer. Further, Castro refused to honor the draft for 3,000 francs ($600) that Louis Huth had put into the colonization effort during Castro's year long absence in Europe. Finally, the empresario never transferred title to 8,000 acres of land in Texas that the Huths bought from him in 1843 at the time they made their original business arrangement. When the elder Huth suggested that Castro use his fifty preferred shares of stock in the Antwerp Society as collateral for the debts he owed the Huths, the empresario shrugged the debt off as inconsequential. He promised to settle the obligation in full after February 15, 1847, when the contract officially ended and, as he assured them, everyone involved would have at least a 150 percent profit on their investment in the colonization enterprise.[23]

In addition to the sums owed the Huth family and others in both France and Germany, Castro drew an advance of 30,000 francs ($6,000) from the Antwerp Society as well as 5,300 francs ($1,060) borrowed personally from Guillaume Dhanis. Thus when he arrived in Texas the empresario appeared to be financially well prepared to continue the colonization work. Nevertheless, as one of his first acts upon arriving in the new Lone Star State, he drafted the society for another 30,000 francs. Although there is no proof of it, Ludwig Huth definitely believed that Castro had managed to

[22] William Elliott to Louis Huth, undated, Castro to Louis Huth, May 15, December 1, 1846, Ludwig Huth to Louis Huth, May 26, 1846, Huth Papers.
[23] Ludwig Huth to Louis Huth, April 6, 1846, Huth Papers.

squander the funds on personal matters not pertaining to the colonization work during his long stay at Galveston in the summer of 1846. Wherever the money had gone, the empresario seemed to remain in need of funding for the duration of the colonization project.[24]

The economic problems that continued to plague the enterprise caused severe personality conflicts. Louis Huth began to press Castro for the money he, Huth, had invested in the enterprise during the empresario's absence in Europe the year before. Castro retorted with allegations that Huth had mismanaged the funds at his disposal and had not made a concerted effort to settle colonists on the grant. The dispute reached a climax in mid-November when the empresario removed Huth from any official position with the colonization project. He then assumed sole control of the Texas operation with Theodore Gentilz acting as his assistant.[25]

While casting about for a better means of transport, Castro began to feel the monetary pinch more and more. Because he had drawn so much money against the Antwerp Society account at the beginning of the partnership, officers of that organization were reluctant to advance him more funding. This led to a growing mistrust between the empresario, who regretted the deal he had made in Antwerp, and his new partners, who received, at best, only minimal accounting for funds expended in Texas. Nevertheless, Castro continued the process of developing a ring of villages surrounding the grant.

In order to continue the project Castro hinted to the Antwerp Society that it might get an extension of time on the contract and with this idea he requested more funding. By this time the Belgian investors were decidedly skeptical of the enterprise, which had produced only great expenses and greater promises from the empresario. The Europeans had

[24] Castro to Bishop Odin, January 14, 1846, Odin Papers, Catholic Archives, Diocese of Galveston-Houston; Guillaume Dhanis to Ludwig Huth, April 16, 1846, included in a letter from Ludwig Huth to Louis Huth, April 21, 1847, Ludwig Huth to Albert Huth, July 9, 1847, Huth Papers.

[25] Public Notice of Dismissal of Louis Huth as Castro Colony Agent, no date, Castro to Louis Huth, November 17, 1846, Huth Papers; Castro to Bishop Odin, January 1, 1847, Odin Papers, Catholic Archives, Diocese of Galveston-Houston.

little idea of the problems concerning operations in Texas; furthermore, communications lagged at least two months in arrears. Castro, who was used to proceeding on his own initiative, showed little patience with the slow pace of the situation.[26]

When the empresario concluded that he was not going to receive further funding from his partners, he acted in a characteristically energetic manner. On March 18, 1847, he borrowed $16,000 from John H. Illis, the Galveston merchant who had been serving as receiving agent for the colonization project. The empresario mortgaged 40,000 acres of concession property plus the lots in Castroville as collateral for the loan and continued his operation as before. This was a remarkable act, for Castro had given up all power to conduct such activity when he signed the Antwerp contract. Of course, Europe remained a long way from Texas. Since he justified his actions by claiming that the Antwerp Society was not adequately supporting the project, the articles of partnership were no longer in force. Meanwhile, the people in Antwerp remained unaware of this latest act, which effectively negated the operation of the Society.[27]

By the summer of 1847 the oft-changing fortunes of Henri Castro and his colonization project had reached a new stage. The empresario had acquired help from the Antwerp Society that enabled him to found three villages within the bounds of the grant while at the same time introducing large numbers of settlers into Texas. In the process he abandoned the faithful Louis Huth, who had done so much to hold the project together. As soon as the usefulness of his European partners began to wane, however, he also abandoned them. As the partnership resources began to dry up, he mortgaged the lands in which he was dealing to provide himself fresh funds for completion of the colonization project.

Henri Castro was a complicated personality whose activi-

[26] Castro to Bishop Odin, December 28, 1846, January 14, 1847, Odin Papers, Catholic Archives, Diocese of Galveston-Houston; Ludwig Huth to Louis Huth, April 21, July 24, 1847, Huth Papers.

[27] Contract between the Société de Colonisation Europée-Américain au Texas and John J. Illis with Henri Castro acting as agent for the Société, Book T2, 119–21, Deed Records, Bexar County Clerk's Office, Bexar County Courthouse, San Antonio.

ties have been described in conflicting ways. There is no doubt
he used unethical, if not illegal, business practices, to achieve
his ends. His correspondence indicates that he believed he
was doing fine work for his fellow man. With that in mind he
continued his colonization work with an unswerving single-
mindedness. Perhaps his vision of great profits to be gained
at any cost was rationalized by the thought that his work would
benefit the colonists he transported to Texas. He thought of
himself as a great man who would receive his due recogni-
tion once he completed his great project.

CHAPTER VI

The Colonists:
Adapting to a New Life

THE formal operation of Castro's contract ended on February 15, 1847, when the legal time limit lapsed. Any potential settlers who had not arrived in Texas by that time could not claim free land under the terms of the contract. Although the empresario had transported more than 2,000 colonists to Texas, no more than 500 or 600 lived in the four villages at the time of the expiration of the contract. The others either resided elsewhere in the state or had returned to their homeland. Those who stayed on the grant faced great physical hardship combined with the necessity of adapting to their new environment. They managed to overcome drought, disease, an unfamiliar land, and frequent dangers to produce a unique adaptation of European cultural elements to an American environment.[1]

When Henri Castro began recruiting colonists, he had in mind farmers capable of settling the frontier. He began recruiting in central France, changed to the Rhine area, and later included many of the German states in the project. The settlers he transported to Texas ultimately included people from France, the German states, Belgium, Holland, Hungary, England, and Mexico.[2]

[1] Herman Seele, *The Cypress and Other Writings of a German Pioneer in Texas,* trans. by Edward C. Breitenkamp, 14–15; Julia Nott Waugh, *Castroville and Henry Castro, Empresario,* 11.

[2] Ships' Lists, Colonization Papers, Archives, Texas State Library, Austin.

In addition to recruiting from a wide range of nationalities the empresario was forced to accept settlers with diverse occupations rather than selecting only farmers as he
had hoped. When he began recruiting potential frontier
farmers in 1842 Castro quickly discovered that they were not
so easily found. He concluded that, "Farmers in easy circumstance rarely emigrate and this remark applies to France
more than any other country."[3] Thus the first settlers he recruited included many nonfarmers from various provinces
within France. As late as 1850 only sixty-one individuals, or
40 percent of the 177 heads of households within the colony,
listed themselves as farmers. The ships lists also bear out this
limited percentage of farmers, particularly in the 1842 and
1843 sailings.[4]

In addition to the problem of recruiting farmers as potential settlers, the empresario found he could fulfill his contract only by sending many settlers to Texas who were without
substantial financial resources. This aspect of the recruiting
technique proved particularly unfortunate because Texas
officials repeatedly warned the empresario to make sure that
all colonists sent to the republic had resources to support
themselves for at least one year. It is understandable that
people in poor financial circumstances were more likely to
emigrate, but the empresario ignored a mandate to provide
for them.[5]

The first group that arrived in Texas on New Year's Day

[3] Castro to Anson Jones, December 8, 1842, Colonization Papers.

[4] U.S. Seventh Census (1850), Schedule I: Free Inhabitants, Medina County;
Ships' Lists for *Ebro, Lyons, Louis Philippe, Jean Key, Henrich, Ocean, Jeanette Marie,*
Colonization Papers.

[5] Sam Houston to William Henry Daingerfield, April 9, 1842, in Amelia W.
Williams and Eugene C. Barker, eds., *The Writings of Sam Houston,* III: 20; Anson
Jones to Ashbel Smith, June 21, 1843, Ashbel Smith to Anson Jones, September 19,
1843, William Daingerfield to Ashbel Smith, November 8, 1843, in George P. Gar-
rison, ed., *Diplomatic Correspondence of the Republic of Texas,* II: 1452, 1464, 1475;
Ashbel Smith to Anson Jones, December 30, 1843, Texas, Department of State
Copybooks of Diplomatic Correspondence, 1836–1846, Letters Received, Archives,
Texas State Library, Austin, 441; William Kennedy to Lord Aberdeen, September 9,
1844, in Ephraim Douglass Adams, *British Diplomatic Correspondence Concerning the
Republic of Texas,* 356–62.

of 1843 most clearly reflects the lack of planning in the early days of the project. They arrived in Texas totally unprepared both financially and psychologically for the frontier experience they faced. Virtually without leadership or guidance, they suffered numerous fatalities from coastal fevers combined with the hardships and exposure caused by their destitute condition. Evidently the empresario believed that the Republic of Texas would care for these people and place them in possession of their property. When this proved false Castro left the colonists to their own devices. It soon became apparent that the French colonists could not fend for themselves without strong leadership.

Members of that first group found themselves stranded in Galveston in January of 1843 without the means of proceeding to the colony. If it had not been for the assistance of Bishop Odin, who advanced them the money to travel to San Antonio, and Sam Houston, who made quarters available to them after they arrived at San Antonio, it is doubtful that many members of the group would have survived. A disaster of that magnitude would have ended the colonization project at that point. Even with help the 1843 colonists suffered many hardships from the unusually wet and cold winter that year. Furthermore, the group became aware of the dangers of travel in Texas when newly married Claude Laurent drowned near Harrisburg en route to Lavaca Bay.[6]

Once these colonists arrived in San Antonio, they found they could not take possession of their lands. The entire country between San Antonio and the Rio Grande River where the grant lay was a no-man's-land where roving bands of Indians, bandits, and occasional parties of Mexican soldiers held sway. The Republic of Texas had neither the time, the manpower, nor the inclination to protect the European

---

[6] William Kennedy to Lord Aberdeen, September 9, 1844, in Adams, *British Correspondence*, 360; Odin to France, February 15, 1843, Jean Marie Odin Papers, Catholic Archives of Texas, Austin; Sam Houston to Major George T. Howard, January 24, 1842, in Williams and Barker, *Writings*, III: 440–41; Jean Marie Odin, Journal, 1842–43, typescript, Diocesan Records, Diocese of Galveston-Houston, Houston.

immigrants while the newcomers tried to establish themselves on their granted properties.[7]

Meanwhile, Castro worked to upgrade his entire operation. He began a concerted effort to recruit more qualified farmers who were at the same time financially able to cope with life in the new country. He changed his recruiting territory to the Alsace region of France where he expected to be more successful. Along with the geographic change he also appointed Louis Huth to manage the Texas operation in order to give it more stability.

Despite this change in management, Castro achieved little success in getting the colonization program on a firm basis until he arrived in Texas in 1844 and established Castroville in the vicinity of the grant. With a town for the colonists the operation assumed greater legitimacy. Nevertheless, the financial situation of the colonists remained poor throughout the remainder of the colonization period.

After Castro returned to Europe in 1845 and reorganized the operation, the number of colonists increased dramatically. Again the area of recruitment changed. The post-1845 emigration tended to center on the Alsace region, with significant numbers of colonists arriving from Switzerland as well as various German states. The Antwerp Society recruited a larger proportion of farmers who fitted better the mold needed to settle the grant. Despite the increased ability to get experienced farmers for the project, the organization still could not get significant numbers of financially able people to go to Texas.[8]

Several factors contributed to the poor financial status of

[7]Linn to Lamar, September 21, 1839, Neal to Lamar, July 1, 1840, in Garrison, *Correspondence*; Angelo Causici vs. J. B. LaCoste and Albert Huth, Fall Term, Bexar County District Court, 1856, Bexar County Archives, Bexar County Courthouse, San Antonio. The failure of the republic to assist the colonists is made clear by the repeated unsuccessful attempts Castro made to get the government to assist in the founding of Castroville. Additionally, most Texans did not want colonists different from them in custom and language in the country as pointed out by Kennedy to Lord Aberdeen, September 6, 1845, in Adams, *British Correspondence*, 548, and in the Houston *Telegraph and Texas Register*, January 22, 1845.

[8]Castro to Louis Huth, November 15, 1843, Ferdinand Louis Huth, Papers, Barker Texas History Center, University of Texas at Austin; Analysis of Ships' Lists, Colonization Papers, Archives, Texas State Library, Austin.

the colonists. To begin with, a large percentage of the Alsatian farmers rented, rather than owned, their property in Europe and thus could not accumulate the amount of cash necessary to tide them over for a year of living in Texas. These farmers' situation became even more critical around 1846 when poor crops combined with a general increase in rents contributed to their indebtedness. Because of their deteriorating financial condition, many of the Alsatian farmers, who were becoming desperate, seized the opportunity to emigrate if the colonization company would pay their fare to the colony. This desire to leave a poor economic situation was offset by the tendency of the Europeans to look on the colonization project as some sort of illegal scheme. To a people used to farms much smaller than 100 acres, the 320- and 640-acre grants offered them in Texas seemed preposterous. They naturally suspected such a fabulous deal that seemingly represented so much wealth.[9]

Most of the colonists originated in the highly populated farming area of the Rhine Valley. The people living there resided in towns and villages and farmed the surrounding countryside. They were accustomed to a stable life-style, well-constructed stone houses, and access to water transportation, although most of them had never traveled farther from home than the nearest large town, which was seldom more than twenty or thirty miles distant.[10]

The circumstances of their life in Europe colored their perceptions of life in Texas. Evidently the prospective colonists were never informed when they arrived at Galveston they still faced a trip of some 200 miles to get to San Antonio, a distance far greater than most of them had traveled in their lifetimes. They believed that upon arriving at Galveston they should be able to take possession of their properties within

[9] Helen Marie Nickel and Patsy Schurchart, "The Christopher Schurchart Family," Schurchart File, James Menke Collection, San Antonio; Ludwig Huth to Louis Huth, May 26, 1846, June 11, 1847, Huth Papers; Ashbel Smith to Anson Jones, December 30, 1842, in Garrison, *Correspondence*, II: 1067.

[10] Taken as a group, the letters written from Ludwig Huth to Louis Huth between 1843 and 1848 in the Huth Papers give an excellent picture of the general situation in Castro's general recruiting area of Europe. For a more general overview consult Oscar Handlin, *The Uprooted*, 7–36.

a few days, since they could not envision traveling much farther.

The agents for Castro in Europe made the trip as easy as possible to avoid confusing the colonists. They arranged all transport and provided detailed instructions on how to leave the country and whom to contact when arriving in New Orleans or Galveston. This proved a difficult process when the project first began because, as Castro said about sea captains, "I could have gotten twenty men for New Orleans to one who was willing to sail for Galveston." As the project continued and the Adelsverein began heavy recruiting in Germany, ships became more available for Texas. Even though the charters became easier to obtain with the passage of time, the ships were all sailing vessels designed for cargo and not for passengers. During the entire period of Castro's colonization project there were no passenger vessels devoted to immigration. Thus the project depended on cargo ships that needed return cargos to assure profit on the trip.[11]

The trip to Texas took from sixty to ninety days depending upon the weather and the condition of the vessel making the voyage although there were a few instances of forty-five day trips. The colonists never found it a pleasant experience. Numerous incidents of sickness and death occurred in addition to the ever-present danger associated with wooden sailing ships of the nineteenth century. The *Carl Wilhelm*, which left Bremen with 130 passengers, arrived off Galveston in July, 1846. While passing through the channel to Galveston Bay the ship grounded and broke up within sight of the town. Only thirty-five passengers survived the wreck. Although the sinking of the *Carl Wilhelm* was unusual, many accidents did happen at sea. Small wonder that most of the colonists arrived in Texas in a dazed and disorganized state of mind.[12]

[11]Odin, Journal; "Société de Colonisation Europée-Américaine au Texas," Menke Collection; A. J. Sowell, *Early Settlers and Indian Fighters of Southwest Texas*, 139; William Kennedy to Lord Aberdeen, December 31, 1845, in Adams, *British Correspondence*, 537; Galveston *Civilian and Galveston Gazette*, January 6, 1846, and June 6, 1851. For an excellent overview of the evolution of immigrant sailing vessels transporting Europeans to the United States see Handlin, *Uprooted*, 37–62.

[12]Sowell, *Settlers*, 97, 114, 141, 155, 159, 170, 181, 347, 368, 375, 783, 811; August Santleben, *A Texas Pioneer*, 1.

Colonists usually began the trip to their property by landing first at Galveston. From there they were transported to Lavaca Bay by shallow draft vessels. Leaving Lavaca Bay, they traveled overland by oxcart to San Antonio and then the twenty-five miles to Castroville. This route varied from time to time as when the ocean-going vessels bypassed Galveston and went directly to Lavaca Bay. At other times, particularly in the first two years, vessels landed at New Orleans where the colonists transferred to the regular packet boat for Galveston and then on to Lavaca Bay. On rare occasions some of the colonists traveled from Houston after first landing at Galveston. Late in the project Castro changed some of the routing to Corpus Christi or to Copano Bay and then overland to the colony. Regardless of the routing, the overland leg of the trip took from two weeks to a month depending upon the weather and the condition of the roads.[13]

The entire process proved a frightening experience for the colonists. After the long sea voyage the overland trip took its toll. Many of the colonists contracted coastal fevers, which were sometimes fatal, while diseases such as cholera and pneumonia developed in the crowded and unsanitary staging area at Indianola on Lavaca Bay. On more than one occasion colonists met with Indians during the overland trip, but only one death—that of young Ziliac Rhin in the 1844 contingent—was attributed to conflict with Indians.

By the time they arrived at Castroville the colonists suffered from exhaustion as a result of the physical rigors of their experience, even if they had an uneventful trip. They faced the reality of beginning a new life in a frontier environment. The only settlement between San Antonio and the Rio Grande, Castroville offered few comforts. Its population was sparse and the land was far from the most fertile. Although some danger existed from Indian raids, coping with the environment presented a much greater threat. Many threw up

[13]"Texas Letters and Documents," *Texana*, 6, no. 4: 374; Notes of Bertha Brauer Griffen, Ihnken File, Menke Collection; "Notes of W. G. Poehler," Poehler File, Menke Collection, "The Wipff Family," Wipff File, Menke Collection; Ships' Lists, Colonization Papers; *Lacoste Ledger* December 8, 1922; Odin, Journal; Contract between James Powers and Henry Castro, November 21, 1846, Fitzsimon Papers, Amarillo Public Library.

their hands and returned to San Antonio or Galveston or Victoria where there were other people and one could feel safe.[14]

Castro brought 2,134 people to Texas during the entire project.[15] But he never convinced more than 1,000 to live in or near the grant at any given time. The adjustments to the new life simply seemed too great. The empresario worked diligently to make the transition from a settled European life-style to living on the frontier as easy as possible for the colonists. He forced the settlers to live in a village situation rather than on isolated homesteads so that they could have the advantage of group protection while maintaining a semblance of their European life-style.[16]

The colonists who remained with the project coped as best they could with an unfamiliar environment. Shelter became the first priority. In each settlement the colonists used materials at hand to build homes. The first structures varied

[14] Fritz Rothe to Relatives in Germany, December 18, 1854, Rothe File, Menke Collection; Ludwig Huth to Louis Huth, February 28, 1845, Huth Papers; Henri Castro, Journal, 115–116, Henri Castro Papers, Barker Texas History Center, University of Texas at Austin; Wipff File, Menke Collection.

[15] Because of the absence of complete ships' lists there is no accurate enumeration of the number of colonists Castro brought to Texas. The number introduced by the empresario was estimated at 5,200 by his son, Lorenzo Castro, in his book *Immigration from Alsace-Lorraine: A Brief Sketch of Castro's Colony in Western Texas*, which was written in an attempt by the younger Castro to start another colonization program. Both Henderson K. Yoakum, *History of Texas from Its First Settlement in 1685 until Annexation to the United States in 1846*, II: 436, and Dudley Wooten, ed., *A Comprehensive History of Texas*, I: 825, give the number of colonists as 600 families, which is the stated number of families in the 1842 contract, but bears little relation to the actual colonization work. Over the years others have given numbers to the project, usually in terms of numbers of families and single men introduced. Both a contemporary of Castro, Herman Seele, in *The Cypress*, 14–15, and a very careful researcher, Julia Nott Waugh, in *Castroville*, used the figure 2,134 as the total number of persons introduced by Castro into Texas. This is the same figure that Castro used in his *Memorial of Henry Castro, Founder of Castro's Colony, to the Senate and House of Representatives of the State of Texas*, and is by far the most accurate. My calculations were made by matching known ships' lists with land-certificate holders and estimating the number of unknown arrivals by using the ratio of arrivals on ships' lists who got land to people not on ships' lists who got land and then applying that ratio to the total persons on the ships' lists to arrive at a total number of colonists introduced into Texas by Castro of 2,075 individuals. That number varies approximately 3 percent from that claimed by Castro in his memorial and gives a fair check on his claim.

[16] Louis Huth, "Account of the Founding of Quihi," Huth Papers, undated; Jesse Sumpter, "Life of Jesse Sumpter, The Oldest Living Citizen of Eagle Pass, Texas" (1902), Barker Texas History Center, University of Texas at Austin.

considerably in size and shape, but they all employed some sort of log construction. Many settlers built picket-type structures composed of small logs set vertically on a log base and chinked the cracks between the pickets with a combination of mud and grass. Others, particularly the Swiss colonists who had considerable woodworking experience in their homeland, constructed what are usually considered traditional log cabins with notched corners using a peculiar technique brought from Europe. Still others built various kinds of lean-to shelters that were constructed over pits in a manner similar to the half dugouts on the Texas plains in the post–Civil War era. All the structures in that early period had thatched roofs made from local bear grass. Regardless of the type of construction, the earliest homes of the colonists were of a primitive nature designed to offer immediate protection from the elements.[17]

The more affluent members of the colony had homes built of wood and stone from the earliest period. Henri Castro, Louis Huth, and a few others built homes of stone in Castroville beginning as early as 1844. Evidence exists that Hispanic laborers from San Antonio built some of the very first Castroville structures of adobe brick. These evidently were not well accepted by the colonists and no mention of them appears beyond the first days of the colony in 1844. Castroville, the principal town of the entire enterprise, set the pattern for the types of permanent structures built in the area, although as late as 1848 a newcomer to the town described it as "a collection of huts of every shape and size."[18]

As the economic condition of the colonists began to improve, their housing reflected the improved situation. The Castro colony developed a distinctive architectural style simi-

[17] Sowell, *Settlers*, 444, 554; Abbe Jean Perrichon, *Vie de Monsiegneau Dubuis, l'Aporte du Texas*, 46; Terry Jordan, *Texas Log Buildings: A Folk Architecture*, 43; Abbe Emmanuel Domenech, *Missionary Adventures in Texas and Mexico, A Personal Narrative of Six Years' Sojourn in Those Regions*, trans. unknown, 65; Ozona *Kicker*, March 26, 1927.

[18] Unsigned printed document from a magazine, H. E. Haass Papers, Texas Collection; Agreement between Henri Castro and Louis Huth, November 20, 1844, Huth Papers; Castro, Journal; Melinda Rankin, *Texas in 1850*, 188–89; Domenech, *Missionary*, 46.

lar to the rural structures in Alsace. Father Claude Marie Dubuis, who became the first permanent priest at Castroville in 1847, is usually given credit for building the first such structure, which was completed in August of 1847. These homes became common in the area by the mid-1850s. They are characterized by a rectangular shape and an unusual roof line that presents a steep gable effect with the front short and the rear long. They also exhibit angular or battered chimney tops with flues rising within the walls. Thus there is no exterior evidence of chimneys other than the tops. The chimneys are also unusual in that they appear at strange places, such as directly over a window because the flues are seldom vertical, but rise at various angles within the walls.

The homes are characteristically built of rough cut stone or some combination of stone and timber that is covered with a lime plaster to give the structure a smooth surface. Two-story houses have ground floors of stone and upper floors of vertical timbers very similar to European construction. The houses all have wooden dormer and casement windows although there are few exterior openings in the structures. In the early days these substantial homes had thatched roofs just like the less-imposing structures. But these soon were replaced with locally made cypress shingles as shingle making rapidly became one of the few money-making activities open to the settlers.[19]

Architecture became possibly the most visible reminder of the place of origin of the Castro colonists, but other more intangible things loomed large in their consciousness. Religion definitely held a place of importance. Castro understood from the beginning of the project the importance of gaining the confidence and assistance of religious leaders to make the colony a success. He emphasized this priority when he persuaded Bishop Odin to dedicate St. Louis Church in

[19]Dubuis to Priest in France, October 25, 1847, H. E. Haass, Papers, Texas Collection, Baylor University, Waco; Terri Ross, "Alsatian Architecture in Medina County," in *Built in Texas*, Francis Edward Abernethy, ed., 121–29; Sowell, *Settlers*, 115.

1844 and later when he became involved in the Pfanner fiasco. Although he prodded Huth to get the church building finished, it was not completed until November 9, 1846. Just a couple of months after the completion of the church Father Claude Marie Dubuis arrived as a missionary to Texas as the first permanent priest at Castroville.[20]

Castro applauded the arrival of the priest to look after the spiritual needs of the colonists; however, his arrival to promote traditional religious activities was not totally supported by the colonists. They represented a diverse group speaking several languages and many times were at odds with one another. The priest was aghast at the babel of languages he encountered in his prospective flock; communication with them was a virtual impossibility. His inability to speak either German or the Alsatian dialect combined with the colonists' sad experience with Father Pfanner only two years earlier caused the colonists to welcome the priest less than cordially. Additionally, the colonists were so preoccupied with day-to-day survival in their precarious frontier situation that religious aspects of their lives received a secondary consideration.[21]

Dubuis, a forceful man, used Castroville as a base of operations and served Quihi, Vandenburg, and Dhanis as well as the Adelsverein towns of Fredericksburg and New Braunfels. Within weeks he mastered the languages well enough to communicate with the parishioners, which thawed their negative attitude. By late spring he expressed particular pride in the faithfulness of the Castroville Catholics and commented favorably on those at the newer towns of Vandenburg and

    [20] Castro, Journal; Waugh, *Castroville*, 46; Austin *Texas Democrat*, February 20, 1847; Houston *Telegraph and Texas Register* March 29, 1847; Victor Bracht, *Texas in 1848*, trans. by Charles Frank Schmidt, 103; Mary Angela Fitzmorris, *Four Decades of Catholicism in Texas, 1820–1860*, 68; Diocesan Records, Diocese of Galveston-Houston, Houston; see also Sister Mary Xavier Holsworthy, "History of the Diocese of Corpus Christi, Texas" (Master's thesis, St. Mary's University, San Antonio), 17.
    [21] Father Dubuis to Priest in France, October 25, 1847, H. E. Haass Papers, Texas Collection. For a good discussion of the state of the colonists at the time of the arrival of Dubuis see Theodore Gittinger, "A History of St. Louis Catholic Church of Castroville, Texas" (Master's thesis, Sam Houston State University, 1972).

Dhanis who were attending mass regularly. Response became so encouraging that Dubuis began a larger stone church, where he celebrated the first mass on Easter Sunday of 1850.[22]

The population of Castro's colony has been estimated as overwhelmingly Catholic in a ratio of five to one. Although this is a reasonably accurate approximation, it does not entirely describe the makeup of the colony. Castroville, which was almost entirely Catholic and Alsatian, set the tone for the colony. Quihi contained a combination of Alsatians and people from the western and northern German states, but the settlers there were predominantly Lutheran. Vandenburg is a little more difficult to categorize, although Dubuis referred to it as having several faithful Catholic families. Dhanis, the town last settled, was overwhelmingly Catholic, but the population there originated almost entirely in the German states of Bavaria and Wurtenburg. Thus the entire colony, which at first glance appears Alsatian and Catholic, actually contained diverse elements within its body.[23] This diversity became greater when, in the early 1850s, Verde Creek on which Vandenburg was built became dry. The loss of the village water supply forced most of those living there to move. A few hardy souls stayed around for a time, hauling their water from the lake at Quihi, but most of the Vandenburg settlers moved a few miles downstream where there was still water and formed the town of New Fountain. Within a relatively short time a German Methodist circuit rider approached the New Fountain people and by 1858 they had built a Methodist

[22] Perrichon, *Dubuis*, 79–80; Father Dubuis to Bishop Odin, April 29, 1847. Castroville Papers, Catholic Archives of Texas, Austin; Dubuis to Priest in France, October 25, 1847, H. E. Haass Papers, Texas Collection; Diocesan Records, Diocese of Galveston-Houston; San Antonio *Southern Messenger*, May 30, 1895; Domenech, *Missionary*, 190.

[23] Waugh, *Castroville*, 1–44; Quantification for Castroville, Quihi, Vandenburg, and Dhanis was derived from a combination of sources. The U.S. Seventh Census (1850), Schedule I: Free Inhabitants, Medina County, Texas combined with the Ships' Lists, Colonization Papers, were used to determine the place of origin and the Texas residence of individuals. Then the Parish Register for St. Louis Catholic Church at Castroville, records of Bethlehem Lutheran Church at Quihi, and the Parish Register for St. Dominic's Catholic Church at Dhanis were used to determine the religious orientation of the colonists listed in the census and on the ships' lists. Dubuis to Odin, April 29, 1847, Castroville Papers, Catholic Archives of Texas.

Church. The activity of evangelistic Protestant denomina-
tions like the Methodists caused the Castroville priests,
Dubuis and Domenech, considerable consternation. They
had experience with the Lutherans in Europe, but they simply
could not understand the proselytizing Methodists, whom
they railed against at length.[24]

Meanwhile, in 1852 the Quihi settlement established
a Lutheran congregation, which in 1854 built the Bethlehem
Lutheran Church. This church, pastored by Rev. Christian
Oefinger, became a rallying point for Lutherans in that part
of the grant. In 1852 the Zion Lutheran congregation also
organized at Castroville, with an initial membership of only
twelve individuals, including Louis Huth. Reverend Oefinger
also pastored this congregation.[25]

These Protestant activities point up the stabilization of
the colonies in the early 1850s as minority religious groups
within the colony began to express themselves. While this activity was taking place, the people at Dhanis undertook construction of the second Catholic church in the colony. They
built St. Dominic's Catholic Church, a log structure, sometime
in 1847 or 1848 as a place the missionary priests from Castroville could conduct religious services when they reached
the settlement. The twenty-five miles to Castroville was simply too far for the colonists to travel to attend church. Later,
in 1853, when they had a sufficiently large population and
times were better, they built a small stone church that served
as a mission until 1868, when they received their first permanent priest.[26]

The Catholic church at Castroville also helped establish

[24] Sowell, *Settlers*, 542–43; Leinweber File, Weimers File, Menke Collection;
A. B. Brucks, "History of New Fountain Methodist Church," New Fountain File,
Menke Collection; Hondo *Anvil-Herald*, May 6, 1976, and August 30, 1978; Macum
Phelan, *A History of Early Methodism in Texas*, 354, 369–70, 429; Domenech, *Mission-
ary*, 59–61.

[25] Hondo *Anvil-Herald*, August 1, 1947, June 25, October 8, October 10, 1952,
March 13, 1953, and May 6, 1976; *125th Anniversary of the Bethlehem Lutheran Church:
Quihi, Texas, 1852–1977; Lest We Forget: Centennial Celebration of the Bethlehem
Lutheran Church, Quihi, Medina County, Texas: October 12, 1952*; Church Records, Zion
Lutheran Church, Castroville, Texas.

[26] Hondo *Anvil-Herald*, August 1, 1947; Josie R. Finger, *125th Anniversary, St.
Dominic's Catholic Church, Old D'Hanis, Texas.*

a school. Shortly after Dubuis arrived in the town, the priest created a school which soon had an enrollment of 70 students. Dubuis, along with Father Chazelle who arrived late in 1847, shared teaching duties, but that activity combined with their regular missionary work proved too great a burden both physically and financially for them to continue alone. They appealed to Castro for assistance with the school.

The empresario agreed that a school was needed. Accordingly he hired a teacher who was fluent in German, French, and English. The school, as Castro visualized it, remained independent of the church and was supported by donations from the colonists. This decision did not particularly please the priests who wanted to continue religious training through the medium of the school. But the clerics became more horrified when Castro hired a Lutheran teacher. The entire school situation caused a tremendous furor within the colony. After some months of heated exchange on the question the priests once more assumed control of the educational activities at Castroville. While this imbroglio continued, no other schools existed in the area. Indeed, as late as 1850 the only other educational activity took place at Dhanis, where a school teacher tutored local children on a part-time basis.[27]

All this activity during the first ten years of the colony indicates that the colonists managed to adapt to their new life-style, but questions of religion and education were of minor concern when compared to physical survival. Agriculture formed the only means of livelihood for the bulk of the colonists. Castro managed to bring significant numbers of farmers to Texas. Once they arrived, the farmers faced several problems. Their immediate concern was acquiring land capable of growing crops. The twenty- and forty-acre plots at Castroville and later at the outlying villages answered this need. These lands all lay in close proximity to water,

[27] Odin to Society for the Propagation of the Faith, April 9, 1847, Odin Papers, Catholic Archives of Texas, Austin; Father Dubuis to Bishop Odin, April 29, 1847, Castro to Bishop Odin May 4, October 9, 1847, Diocese of Galveston-Houston; U.S. Seventh Census (1850), Schedule I: Free Inhabitants, Medina County; Finger, *125th Parish Anniversary, St. Dominic's Catholic Church.*

which allowed farming activity, but the bulk of the land was not so favorably situated and did not lend itself easily to agriculture. By the mid-1850s the colonists were rapidly adopting stock raising, a pursuit much better suited to the land.[28]

In the first days of the colony, even with the assignment of decent agricultural properties, the colonists faced difficulties in starting a new life. Castro soon recognized that priority lay with getting a crop in during the first year the colonists were on the land. He emphasized that they must clear land and plant crops even before attempting to build homes. As a result all the early homes in the area have a temporary quality. At that point the lack of funds and farming equipment of the colonists came into play. They simply did not have the equipment to begin farming, so Castro furnished draft animals, tools, and seed to start farms. When it became obvious that farming techniques used in Europe could not be applied, the empresario hired Texans to assist the colonists.[29]

Creating farms proved a difficult process. The land had to be cleared by hand, and most of the plowing and planting was done with hoes and shovels. A food supply depended on getting the crops planted. Despite the diverse experiments of Castro, who planted all kinds of vegetables near his Castroville home, the main crop of the colonists became corn, which was new to them. Even killing deer, turkey, and other game plentiful in the area was impossible for most colonists because they had no guns. Once again Castro hired local people to hunt game and supply the colonists with meat during the establishment period of the colony.[30]

The dangers from natural calamities peaked in 1849

[28] San Antonio *Texas Sun*, March 4, 1880; *Lacoste Ledger*, December 8, 1922; Angelo Causici vs. J. B. Lacoste and Albert Huth, Bexar County District Court, Fall Term, 1856, Bexar County Archives; U.S. Seventh Census (1850), Schedule IV: Agriculture, Medina County, Texas.

[29] Castro to Louis Huth, February 6, 11, 18, 1845. Huth Papers; Castro, Journal; Houston *Telegraph and Texas Register*, November 6, 1844; Castro to Louis Huth, unsigned and undated instructions, Huth Papers.

[30] Sowell, *Settlers*, 182, 447, 811–12; Hondo *Anvil-Herald* January 16, 1953; Castro, Journal; Castro to Louis Huth, unsigned and undated instructions, Huth Papers; Bracht, *Texas*, 101; Domenech, *Missionary*, 50–51, 55; Louis Huth on Founding of Quihi, undated, Huth Papers; "Jesse Sumpter," Barker Texas History Center.

when the colony suffered the severe blow of a drought. For more than eighteen months, beginning in late 1848 and continuing on into 1850, almost no rain fell in the region. The lack of rain caused the Medina River to dry up and all crops failed during 1849. This forced many colonists to leave the confines of the colony at least temporarily, if for no other reason than simply to find food.[31]

Even if a crop was harvested, few of the colonists had the means to transport their produce to market. Most of the people at Quihi, Vandenburg, and Dhanis had to walk to Castroville or San Antonio if they had business in either town. Colonists often walked the more than thirty miles from Quihi to a mill near San Antonio carrying bags of corn to be ground into corn meal for food. This was a necessity, for during the first years of the colony many people lived on a diet of corn-meal mush supplemented by some garden vegetables and wild game.[32]

It was a struggle for the colony to survive in the face of the difficulties of establishing a new life on the frontier. Accidents like rattlesnake bites, broken bones, burns, and disease took a considerable toll. One family of six at Vandenburg perished when they gathered and ate some wild greens that turned out to be poisonous plants. Because the Europeans were unfamiliar with the environment and with methods of determining direction in an uncharted region they frequently wandered off and became lost, which usually resulted in illness from exposure and on some occasions even death. John Grossenbacher and his daughter Barbara left Dhanis one day to fish in the creek. They became confused about direction and wandered around lost for fourteen days. The two managed to survive on bird eggs and a fawn they found. Ultimately a band of friendly Indians found the Grossenbachers and returned them to the settlement little the worse for wear. Their escapade ended happily, but several colonists disappeared, never to be seen alive again.[33]

    [31] J. E. Watkins, unknown Houston newspaper, 1930, Menke Collection; Hondo *Anvil-Herald*, January 16, 1953, and July 22, 1949.
    [32] Sowell, *Settlers*, 115–16; J. E. Watkins, unknown Houston newspaper, 1930, Menke Collection.
    [33] Domenech, *Missionary*, 55; Sowell, *Settlers*, 448.

Then, to further complicate matters, a cholera epidemic struck Texas in the spring of 1849. The disease, which ran its course in about six weeks in San Antonio, claimed several hundred lives in the Alamo City. The deaths in Castroville began on April 23 and for more than a month someone died almost every day. The official count of Catholic deaths in Castroville numbered sixteen although the total undoubtedly was much higher because of unreported fatalities in the outlying areas of the colony.[34]

Even though the cholera epidemic caused an unusual number of deaths in a short time, diseases of all kinds posed a constant threat. Since Europeans were not accustomed to the high temperatures of Texas, those who arrived in the warmer months suffered much illness. Thus, most ships sailing to Texas were scheduled to arrive in the autumn and winter so the colonists could acclimate better. As the number of immigrants increased, crowded conditions on the ships, at Galveston, and at Indianola accelerated the incidence of death from various diseases. Castro tried to provide medical help to the colonists when he recruited Dr. George Cupples in 1844. Cupples, who served the colony for several years, later moved to San Antonio where he had a long and distinguished medical career. He was replaced in the colony by Dr. John Huffman, who came from Pennsylvania where he recently had emigrated from Switzerland. The presence of a doctor among the colonists provided some assistance, but the incidence of death from disease remained high throughout the early days of the colony.[35]

The highly dramatic and colorful Indian threat to the colonists proved to be based more on rumor and sensationalist newspaper accounts than fact. When Castroville was established in 1844, a band of Lipan Apaches camped along the Medina River below the townsite. In the early days these people often came into the town and traded with the settlers.

[34] Sowell, *Settlers*, 171; "Leinweber Family History," Leinweber File, Seiver File, Menke Collection; Hondo *Anvil-Herald*, January 16, 1953; Parish Register, St. Louis Catholic Church.

[35] Ships' Lists, Colonization Papers; Bollaert, *Bollaert's Texas*, 221; Houston *Telegraph and Texas Register*, May 13, June 20, 1846; Pat Ireland Nixon, *A Century of Medicine in San Antonio Texas*, 168; Huffman File, Menke Collection.

They brought venison and hides while they received various foodstuffs and beads in return. The settlers dealt most often with the Lipans, but occasionally they were visited by bands of Kickapoos and Comanches.[36]

Castroville itself, despite the numerous entreaties of Castro to government officials and the near hysterical fears of the colonists, never faced imminent danger from Indian attack. The settlers, newly arrived from Europe, had few firearms or any experience in handling guns. With this almost total lack of self-protection, tales of events like the 1840 Comanche raid in the Victoria area naturally made them apprehensive. From time to time Capt. Jack Hays and his ranger company scouted in the area, but no ranger company was permanently based there. After the death of the Brinkhoff family at Quihi in March of 1846, Capt. John Conner formed a ranger company on July 31, 1846 that was stationed on the Medina above Castroville. At least six younger members of the colony joined that company and gained valuable experience in maintaining frontier defense. Conner's rangers, including the colony volunteers, joined the regular army and served in the Mexican War beginning in the fall of 1846. This left the area without an immediate defense force, although the period of the Mexican War resulted in most Indians staying out of the area because of the many soldiers at various places in the region.[37]

Most of the Indian incidents during the early days of the colony involved investigations of the new settlements by curious bands or horse theft, which was a way of life with nomadic plains tribes. In the first days of the Dhanis settlement a group of seventy Comanches arrived and wandered among the rude shelters the colonists were erecting. Fearing the worst, some of the settlers who were cooking offered the Indians food to placate them. The Indians ate all the cooked

[36] Sowell, *Settlers*, 98, 114, 162, 554; J. E. Watkins, unknown Houston newspaper, 1930, Menke Collection.

[37] Castro, Journal; Sowell, *Settlers*, 99, 143, 160–61, 182–84, 348–49, 369–71, 447, 559, 812; Executive Record Book, 1846–47, no. 76: 54–55, Archives, Texas State Library, Austin; Habe File, Menke Collection; San Antonio *Texas Sun*, March 4, 1880.

food, appropriated the uncooked supplies, and took other goods from the hapless colonists. They left in a high good humor.[38]

Dhanis and Quihi, as smaller outlying settlements some distance from San Antonio, experienced most of the Indian visits. One of the more frightening incidents took place in March of 1848 when a combined band of Lipans and Kickapoos raided Quihi. They first came upon Blas Meyer, whom they murdered, and then proceeded to the Rudolph Charobiny farm. There they appropriated all the livestock and kidnapped the newly married Francesca Charobiny. After the raiders had traveled a couple of miles, Mrs. Charobiny managed to slip off her captor's horse and run for the protection of a grove of trees. The pursuing Indians wounded her severely with two arrows and when she could not rise they assumed she was dead. Fearing pursuit the Indians quickly rode on, leaving the unfortunate Mrs. Charobiny, who recovered from her wounds although she walked with a severe limp the rest of her life.[39]

By the end of the Mexican War in 1848 the residents of the colony received better protection. A ranger company, commanded by Charles DeMontel, stationed itself on Seco Creek just a mile from Dhanis, while Conner's ranger company returned to the Medina above Castroville. Further, the younger generation of colonists, many of whom served in the United States army in the war, were much better prepared to offer protection against possible Indian raids. Then in July of 1849 the site of the ranger camp on Seco Creek became Fort Lincoln and two companies of United States military personnel were stationed there. Fort Lincoln, until it was abandoned three years later, served as a major deterrent to Indian raids.[40]

In many ways Castro's colonists during the first ten years

[38] See the numerous incidents mentioned throughout Sowell, *Settlers.*
[39] Ibid., 349–447.
[40] U.S. Seventh Census (1850), Schedule I: Free Inhabitants, Medina County, Texas; W. P. Webb, ed., *Handbook of Texas*, I: 628; Sowell, *Settlers*, 184–86, 448; *Frontier Times* (Bandera, Texas), July, 1926, 8; Cornelia and Garland Crook, "Fort Lincoln Texas," *Texas Military History*, 4: 145–61.

of their existence faced more difficulties than others settling on the Texas frontier. They had no experience in the life they were beginning. Most were not farmers, but city dwellers placed in a situation where farming was the main way of life. They came to Texas ill-prepared both psychologically and economically for the work at hand. Yet they gradually overcame the rigors of frontier life as they developed the expertise to survive and in some cases managed even to prosper. They overcame drought, disease, Indian attack, and all the other problems associated with frontier life. Additionally, they developed a unique style of architecture and established a stronghold of Catholicism in their area. By the early 1850s those who stayed had begun to stabilize themselves in their new environment.

CHAPTER VII

The Land: Distributing
the Grant Property

THE fact that 2,134 colonists arrived in Texas before August 15, 1847 to settle on Castro's grant did not mean that they actually occupied the property. At that time no colonists lived on granted land nor had any colonists received legal title to their property. Castroville and the other villages within the confines of the grant all stood on private property and were not subject to the terms of the colonization contract. Getting the State of Texas to honor the terms of the contract proved to be as great a problem as settling the grant. The struggle to get and retain legal possession of the granted land remained a major question from 1842 until its final disposition in 1855.[1]

The entire Castro colony project rested upon the promise of land. In 1842 the Republic of Texas had used its enormous land resources as a lever to promote defense and economic growth. Castro and his associates seized on the idea of free land as a means to gain great wealth. The colonists wanted the land for numerous reasons ranging from the desire for adventure to a need for a means of establishing a secure future for a family. Whatever their reasons for seeking the public lands appropriated for Castro's colony, the participants in the drama never fully realized their dreams.[2]

---

[1] Angelo Causici vs. J. B. Lacoste and Albert Huth, Statement of Facts, January 16, 1857, Bexar County Archives, Bexar County Courthouse, San Antonio.

[2] For an excellent discussion of Republic of Texas motivation for granting empresario contracts see Thomas Lloyd Miller, *The Public Lands of Texas.* In the same

The grant, as originally made on February 15, 1842, consisted of two parts. One lay along the Rio Grande. It comprised two portions, each twenty-five miles in length by twenty miles wide, or a total of approximately 600,000 acres. Since no attempt was made to colonize this portion of the grant because of the difficulties with the Mexican government the portion of the grant beginning thirty miles west of San Antonio was the one settled. It contained approximately 1.25 million acres, which encompassed parts of present day Medina, Uvalde, Frio, LaSalle, McMullen, Atascosa, and Bexar counties.[3]

The Republic of Texas planned to use this large block of land as a buffer protecting the approaches to San Antonio from the south and the west. Both the main roads from Laredo and Eagle Pass crossed the grant and large-scale settlement in the area would help deter any invasion force using the highways. Further, most Indian raids in the San Antonio area came from the west, so settlement in that direction would tend to stop those incursions. The grant location was admirably situated for defense of the republic.[4]

This very suitability of the grant for defense purposes, however, created a considerable problem in convincing the colonists that it was an ideal place for settlement. Danger of Mexican invasion or Indian attack loomed large in the imaginations of the colonists. Those worries, combined with the general lack of cooperation from Texas officials in assisting the colonists to assume possession of their property, greatly hampered efficient settlement of the grant. Indeed, not until Castro took personal charge of the operation in 1844 did the Europeans even manage to see the grant, much less take possession of any of their lands. Even then the timid colonists were afraid to leave the protection of Castroville and venture onto the unsettled grant. Meanwhile, the republic offered

vein, almost every letter in the Huth Papers contains some reference to the enormous profits to be made from Castro colony lands by Castro's associates.

[3] The area of the grant was calculated by plotting the grant boundaries on the original ownership maps issued by the General Land Office of Texas and computing the acreage encompassed within the designated boundaries of the grant.

[4] General Land Office of Texas, *Map of Castro's Colony.*

only minimal protection with its small overworked ranger force.[5]

Finally, when the first movement onto the grant was made at Quihi, disaster struck in the form of Indian attack. This confirmed the worst fears of the colonists concerning the fearful nature of the new land, and Louis Huth, acting as agent, was unable to make any headway toward further settlement. Once again Castro with his forceful personality established the last two settlements and made some movement toward settling the grant. Here again the shrewd Frenchman showed his organizational genius as he convinced the colonists that their little villages were the best defense against Indian incursions.[6]

It was vital to Castro's interests that he place colonists on their property. The original colonization law stated that each colonist must live on his property for three years, build a suitable residence, and put fifteen acres under cultivation in order to get legal title to the land. As the difficulties associated with settling the grant became more apparent to legislators, a movement developed to modify residence requirements. Finally, the Texas legislature rescinded the portion of the law requiring residence on the grant. Instead, the colonists only had to prove through two reliable witnesses that Henri Castro introduced them into Texas prior to 15 February 1847.[7]

For the purposes of the republic the grant served admirably, but for the other participants in the project it proved less than ideal. The fewer than fifty families living within the bounds of the grant at the termination date of the contract on February 15, 1847, give mute testimony to this fact. Even those hardy souls were not living on granted land proper. It was not Indians, the hardships, the lack of official coopera-

[5] Henri Castro, Journal, Henri Castro Papers, Barker Texas History Center, University of Texas at Austin; *Courrier d'Alsace*, August 27, 1846, Ferdinand Louis Huth, Papers, Barker Texas History Center, University of Texas at Austin; Julia Nott Waugh, *Castroville and Henry Castro, Empresario*, 58–73.
[6] Sally Redus, "The Life of Mrs. John Redus," Redus File, James Menke Collection, San Antonio.
[7] Austin *Texas State Gazette*, October 27, 1849; H. P. N. Gammel, *The Laws of Texas, 1822–1897*, III: 497.

tion, or the other problems associated with settling the new land that formed the major barrier to settlement; it was the nature of the land itself.[8]

The main grant occupied a region little suited for agriculture as it was practiced in the nineteenth century. The grant, which extended roughly north and south, was traversed on its northern edge by the Balcones Escarpment, which marks the southern extension of the Edwards Plateau. Just below the Balcones Escarpment and crossing the grant from east to west is the southern Blacklands belt. This strip of land, crossed by many small streams originating in the escarpment, provided the only large-scale region within the grant suitable for agriculture. The southern Blacklands are joined in the southern one-third of Medina County by the Coastal Plains soils that also cross the grant from east to west. The coastal soils continue southward and make up the rest of the landforms within the grant. They vary considerably in composition and are not well watered because most of the streams crossing the Blacklands soil belt cease to flow before reaching the coastal soils. Thus even today much of the southern portion of Castro's grant is suitable only for livestock range and wildlife habitat. With only the extreme northern portion of the grant, located in the upper two-thirds of Medina County, suitable for agriculture, the likely area of settlement within the grant was greatly reduced.[9]

In addition to the general geographic distribution of suitable agricultural lands within the grant area, the limited availability of water also retarded settlement. Only a few large streams existed on the grant. By the terms of Castro's contract all lands within the confines of the grant were exclusively reserved for his colonists with the exception of those properties already filed on at the time of the issuance of

[8] Angelo Causici vs. J. B. LaCoste and Albert Huth, Statement of Facts, Bexar County Archives.
[9] Elmer H. Johnson, *The Natural Regions of Texas*, 133–41; Glenn W. Dittmar, Michael L. Dieke, and Davie L. Richmond, *Soil Survey of Medina County, Texas*, 1, 3–4; Jack W. Stevens and Davie L. Richmond, *Soil Survey of Uvalde County, Texas*, 22, 25, 28, 31–32, 43, 47; Glenn W. Dittmar and Jack W. Stevens, *Soil Survey of Atascosa County, Texas*, 1, 41–42, 90; F. B. Taylor and D. L. Richmond, *Soil Survey of Bexar County, Texas*, 1, 4, 6–8.

Castro's contract. Without exception, all the streams within the bounds of the grant, including both Hondo Creek, which runs north and south in the middle of the grant, and the Frio River, which forms its southern boundary, were taken up by previous claimants. This left the Castro colonists without access to lands with surface water, which in turn made it impossible to live in the area.[10]

The physical characteristics of the land caused Castro untold numbers of problems as he tried to convince the colonists to stay on the grant. Providing the twenty- and forty-acre farm plots at Castroville where farming was feasible was partially designed to counteract the adverse effect of the poor quality of concession land. Castro standardized this technique in the later settlements by locating Quihi, Vandenburg, and Dhanis on previously granted lands where water was available. In each of these settlements Castro made cash deals with the owners, divided the property into twenty- and forty-acre plots, and settled his colonists in concentrated European-style villages on the smaller acreages. These villages, all in the arable northern portion of the grant, proved relatively successful. Later plans for the villages of Osy, on Seco Creek south of Dhanis, and San Miguel, on San Miguel Creek in Frio County, never got beyond the planning stage because of the extremely arid nature of that part of the grant.[11]

Despite success in getting the villages established in the grant area, Castro continued to have considerable trouble with the Texas government. It simply would not issue the ac-

[10] Original Property Ownership Maps for Medina, Uvalde, Frio, LaSalle, Atascosa, McMullen, and Bexar Counties, General Land Office of Texas.

[11] Records for the smaller acreages are available in Books A2, A3, A4, A5, A6, A7, A8, A9, A10, A11, A12, and A21 of Medina County Deed Records in the County Clerk's Office at Hondo; there is some confusion as to the exact nature of settlements at Osy and San Miguel. Castro indicates that colonists were living in Osy in several of his letters to Bishop Odin, but Father Pfanner's letter in the Colmar (Germany) *Courrier d'Alsace* on August 27, 1846, indicates that the priest refused to allow his people to be settled at the site. These are the only specific references to that settlement in all the material relating to the colony and it is supposed that Osy existed only in the fertile imagination of the empresario. Laguna San Miguel never got beyond the investigation stage as indicated in Theodore Gentilz, "Voyage a' la Laguna San Miguel, Texas, November 2, 1847," Gentilz-Fretelliere Papers, Daughters of the Republic of Texas Library, San Antonio.

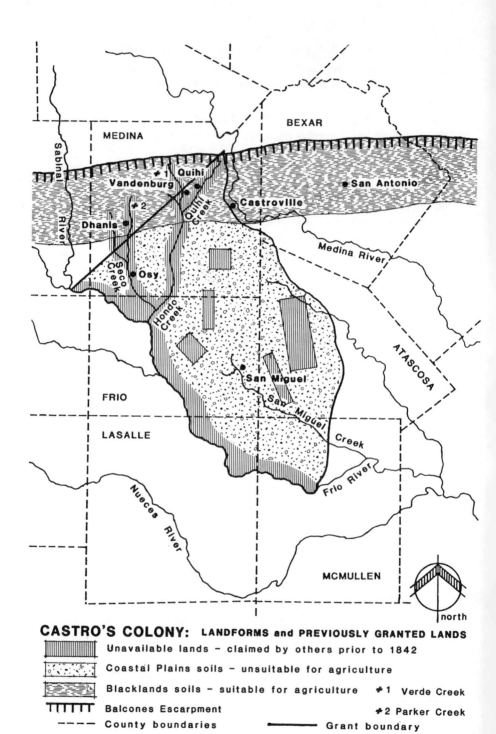

CASTRO'S COLONY: LANDFORMS and PREVIOUSLY GRANTED LANDS

Unavailable lands – claimed by others prior to 1842

Coastal Plains soils – unsuitable for agriculture

Blacklands soils – suitable for agriculture   #1 Verde Creek

⊤⊤⊤⊤⊤ Balcones Escarpment   #2 Parker Creek

– – – – County boundaries   —————— Grant boundary

tual land certificates that would give the colonists legal ownership of their individual grants. Castro first petitioned the legislature in 1844 to furnish the colonists with legal title to the land. He repeated his request at regular intervals. In each instance the empresario went to considerable lengths to explain his sacrifice toward the successful completion of the project.[12]

Finally in January, 1850, John M. Carolan was appointed land commissioner to Castro's Colony. Carolan, an Irish immigrant to the earlier McMullen-McGloin colony, through personal initiative and adroit political skill had held several political offices in Bexar County and the city of San Antonio. His appointment seemed to assure the honest and efficient apportionment of the grant property.[13]

As soon as the appointment was confirmed, Castro began to scurry around the state trying to locate colonists who had left the vicinity of the concession. He traveled to San Antonio, Victoria, Corpus Christi, Lavaca, Galveston, and Houston in a desperate search cajoling and making promises to stray colonists.[14] In addition legal notices of Carolan's schedule appeared in various area newspapers. They read:

Notice:
    The emigrants introduced by H. Castro, under his Colonization contract with the Republic of Texas, are hereby notified that I will be at Castroville on the 3rd day of April, A.D. 1850, to issue certificates to such of the immigrants as are entitled to land under the provisions of the act of the last Legislature of the State of Texas, approved 22nd January, A.D. 1850.

                                        J. M. Carolan Commissioner
                                        Castro's Colony[15]

When Carolan began issuing the certificates Castro was aghast. The papers gave the land directly to the individ-

[12] Memorial of Henry Castro to the Senate and House of Representatives Assembled, 1844, Colonization Papers, Archives, Texas State Library, Austin; both the 1844 and 1855 petitions from Castro to the Texas Congress emphasized Castro's sacrifices to the cause of establishing the colony. Both are located in the Colonization Papers Archives, Texas State Library, Austin.
[13] Gammel, *Laws*, III: 497; Jack C. Butterfield, "The Free State of Bejar," Daughters of the Republic of Texas Library, San Antonio.
[14] Galveston *Civilian and Galveston Gazette*, April 21, 1850.
[15] San Antonio *Western Texan*, April 11, 1850.

ual colonists and not to the empresario to distribute as he thought. This removed the empresario's authority to force the colonists to give him half the property granted them as all had agreed to upon becoming colonists. Henceforth he could only rely upon the goodwill of the individual grantees to honor their agreements.[16]

The commissioner traveled to Castroville where he issued certificates from April 15 to April 25, 1850. Later that year he issued certificates on June 18, October 30 and 31, as well as on November 4 and 5. During 1851 he again issued certificates on February 17 and 21, April 28, June 12, July 23, July 28, and September 8. At that point Carolan closed the books with a total of 360 land certificates in possession of colonists.[17]

Castro was dismayed. This represented only a portion of the people he had introduced into Texas. Once again he petitioned the Texas legislature to issue more certificates. He claimed that the first commissioner did not remain in Castroville long enough to service all the colonists. His persistence yielded results when the legislature appointed another land commissioner to assist the Castro colonists.[18]

This time Tro Ward, assistant district clerk for Bexar County, received the appointment on February 10, 1854. Ward began issuing certificates on April 20 and 21, 1854. He also issued others on May 17, July 13, and August 25 of that same year. In all, Ward issued a total of 125 certificates while serving as land commissioner of the Castro colony, but for some unexplained reason he ceased issuing the certificates before his term expired.[19]

Once again Castro clamored for action toward putting

[16] Gammel, *Laws*, III: 497.

[17] Typescript of Castro Colony Land Certificate Book, H. E. Haass, Papers, Barker Texas History Center, University of Texas at Austin.

[18] Memorial of Henry Castro, Founder of Castro's Colony, to the Senate and House of Representatives of the State of Texas, 1855, Colonization Papers.

[19] The only background information on Tro Ward consists of various documents he signed while acting as assistant district clerk for Bexar County. Evidently Carolon could not serve as land commissioner the second time so his assistant, Tro Ward, was appointed to his place. Henry Castro, Memorial, 1855, Colonization Papers; Castro Colony Certificate Book, Haass Papers, Barker Center.

the colonists in possession of their lands. He succeeded again when on December 26, 1854, Charles N. Riotte, a prominent French immigrant living in San Antonio, was appointed commissioner to replace Ward. Riotte issued his first certificates on January 29 and 30, 1855 and during the last three days of February of that same year he issued others. In all Riotte put seventy-three colonists in possession of their property and ended once and for all land distribution for the Castro grant.[20]

The Castro colony commissioners issued a total of 558 land certificates, but because of several duplications only 546 individuals actually received property. They included 224 single men and 322 married men who were granted a total of 277,760 acres. In addition, Castro received 38,400 acres in premium lands. Thus colonizing Castro's grant cost the Republic of Texas 316,160 acres of public land.[21]

Considering the difficulty that the empresario encountered in the enterprise, he achieved remarkable success in disposing of the property. When he received the 1.25-million-acre concession in 1842, approximately 500,000 acres or some 40 percent already had been granted. This meant that of the remaining 750,000 acres, Castro disposed of approximately 42 percent. This represented a considerable feat, particularly in view of the fact that it contained much of the least desirable land in the concession.[22]

The process by which the certificates were issued is also interesting. Carolan issued 360 certificates to specific individ-

[20] C. N. Riotte to Governor E. M. Pease, January 4, 1855, Colonization Papers; San Antonio *Ledger*, December 9, 1858; Castro Colony Land Certificate Book, Haass Papers, Barker Center.

[21] General Land Office of Texas, Files of Individual Land Holders; *Abstract of All Original Land Titles Comprising Grants and Locations to August 31, 1941* IV: 112–39, 303–33, 567–606, 688–756, 882–922. The original Castro Colony Land Certificate Book has been lost so verification of the colonists' land grants relied on the copy in the Haass Papers, Barker Center. The information in that copy was checked against the *Abstract of Titles* for the seven counties involved in the grant. All the grants were issued as third-class certificates so any third-class certificates left in the *Abstract of Titles* after the known colonists had been eliminated were checked against the original titles in the General Land Office files to verify that all colonists receiving land had been accounted for.

[22] Computed from the original land ownership maps issued by the General Land Office of Texas for Medina, Uvalde, Frio, LaSalle, Atascosa, McMullen, and Bexar Counties.

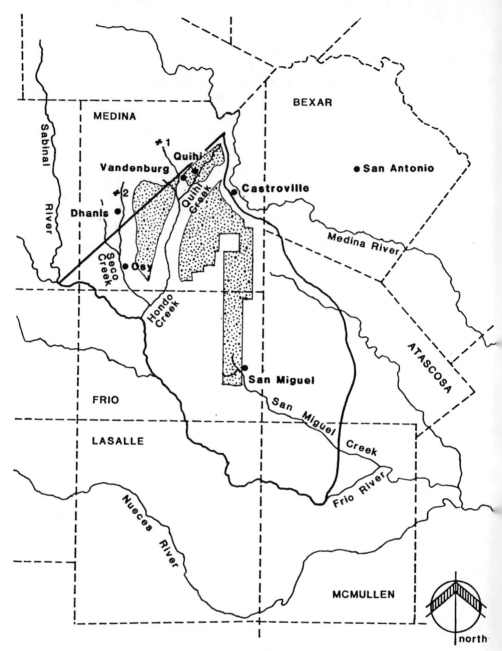

CASTRO'S COLONY:

LANDS GRANTED to CASTRO and HIS COLONISTS

Granted lands   #1   Verde Creek

---- County boundaries   #2   Parker Creek

—— Grant boundary

uals for specific surveys of land on the grant. Of the 125 issued by Ward, however, 16 were floating, that is, they were for some unspecified piece of land within the confines of the grant, and 41 were issued with Angelo Causici as administrator of the estate of the grantee. Causici was justice of the peace for Medina County, and also the grandson of Henri Castro. Of the 73 certificates issued by Charles Riotte, 71 were floating and Causici was administrator for thirteen grantees. It appears that the first 360 certificates went to resident colonists who already had drawn lots for their property and had surveys in hand. After Castro realized the small showing of land claimants, however, he persuaded others from throughout Texas to ask for acreage and managed to get a member of his family, Causici, to oversee those from whom he got powers of attorney. His management appears evident in this particular phase of the land question.[23]

The question of who ultimately received the property brings the entire process into much sharper focus. Initial ownership of the land lay with the colonists in the amount of 277,760 acres. This very quickly changed. By 1859 the amount of land still in the possession of colonists proper fell to only 62,880 acres or 22.6 percent of their original amount. The other 214,880 acres belonged to land speculators. Of that amount at least 150,880 acres either belonged to or had been in the possession of Henri Castro. Among those who garnered part of the land were San Antonio merchants Joseph Ulrich and J. B. LaCoste, who received 12,160 and 9,600 acres respectively. Twelve other men acquired holdings of between 1,280 and 3,840 acres, while Louis Huth who got 2,800 acres, and C. V. Riotte, 640 acres, managed to have a hand in the speculation. The balance of the colony land went to a number of individuals in 320- and 640-acre blocks. It is apparent that Castro proved to be as successful as a land speculator as he was an empresario.

Castro's methods of obtaining the land varied from case to case. Probably as many as 75 percent of the colonists honored their agreements to give him half their property, de-

[23] Castro Colony Land Certificate Book, Haass Papers, Barker Center.

spite the fact that Castro vehemently claimed on numerous
occasions that few of the colonists gave him the land as promised. In other instances he actually purchased the land from
the grantee for sums ranging from ten to twenty dollars per
640-acre section. In one case he traded a bottle of whiskey
for 640 acres. A few individuals simply gave their property to
the empresario because they believed the location and difficulty of using the land made it completely worthless.[24]

This does not mean that the colonists who disposed of
their land did not remain in the vicinity. Many of those who
sold or traded their property preferred to farm the forty-
acre plots near Castroville rather than run the risk of living
in an exposed situation on the grant proper. Indeed, numerous colonists lived on the town lots at Castroville and either
farmed the outlying lands in a manner reminiscent of European practices or worked at various occupations in the village. This seemed to have been the preferred mode of life
for those who remained in the immediate area. The actual
population in the colony region fluctuated considerably depending upon circumstances such as drought, disease,
changing economic conditions, and the addition of later immigrants who either arrived to join a family or were attracted
by kindred Europeans.[25]

Castro's good fortune in acquiring so much land was
relatively short-lived. In 1853 John H. Illis of Houston sued
Castro for the sum of $20,228.43 plus interest and costs, se-
cured by land certificates for much of the colony land. When
the empresario sold his concession to the Belgian businessmen, the new organization hired Illis as its Galveston agent.
During the course of the operation the sum owed Illis and

[24] Survey of deed records for Bexar County at San Antonio, Medina County
at Hondo, Frio County at Pearsall, Uvalde County at Uvalde, LaSalle County at
Cotulla, McMullen County at Tilden, and Atascosa County at Jourdanton; Lorenzo
Castro, *Immigration from Alsace*, 1; "Humbug Property," H. E. Haass Papers, Texas
Collection, Baylor University, Waco; Rev. Roy Rhin to Bobby Weaver, October 1980;
Angelo Gausici vs. J. B. LaCoste and Albert Huth, Statement of Facts, January 16,
1857, Bexar County Archives.
[25] Santleben, *Pioneer*, 1–20; the 1850 census reflects this situation reasonably
well. The census was taken just after a long drouth and the cholera epidemic of
1849 and the census taker noted seventeen vacant houses in Castroville alone.

Company mounted steadily and Castro was forced to sign notes promising payment. When the Belgians realized that they were not going to make the expected profit on their operation and cut off the money supply to Castro, the empresario mortgaged the grant property to get operating money. Later, when Castro was unable to meet the terms of the note, Illis sued.[26]

In one of the largest land suits in early Texas, Illis won a judgment against Castro for hundreds of parcels of land. Castro loudly proclaimed the injustice of the action and made numerous land transfers to his wife, Amelia; his grandson, Angelo Causici; and his son, Lorenzo. The transfer to Amelia is particularly interesting because Castro claimed that upon his marriage to her in 1813 she brought him a dowry of 50,000 francs, which he subsequently spent on the colonization project. Thus, he repaid her with the properties he owned in Texas. Ultimately, Illis received over 120,000 acres of concession land plus all the lots in Castroville to be sold at public auction until he recovered his money. The lots brought $14,869.95, while choice portions of the land yielded $1,719.90 for a total of $16,689.85, which satisfied the lawsuit. The lands not sold at auction were returned to Castro.[27]

This lawsuit left a bad taste in the mouth of many colonists, who maintained that they already had paid Castro for the lots in Castroville and were forced to pay Illis again for the same lots. Although losing the lawsuit struck a considerable blow at his fortunes, Castro managed to retain at least 84,320 acres of the colonists' lands plus the 38,400 acres of premium land, leaving him with holdings of at least 122,720 acres. This acreage managed to keep him in reasonable fi-

[26] Petition of Henry Castro to District Court of Bexar County, April Term, 1848, Bexar County Archives.

[27] "Humbug Property," Haass Papers, Texas Collection; Medina County Deed Records, Book A3: 120–123, Book T2: 2, 8, 10, 12, 16, 106, Book 4: 158, 349, 397, 440, 442, Book 5: 22, 107, 188, 431, Book 6: 20, 84, 169, Medina County Clerk's Office, Hondo; Henry Castro to Angelo Causici in trust for Amelia Mathias, Medina County Deed Records, Book 1, 355; Medina County Deed Records, Book A3, 41–43, 135–40, 159–61.

nancial circumstances for the rest of his life, despite his pro-
testations of having been ruined by the Texas venture.[28]

Meanwhile, Castro continued to badger the colonists for
one-half of their land as stipulated in their original contracts.
Most honored the agreements, but some did not. Ultimately,
the question of the legality of the payment went to court. In
1855 the Supreme Court of Texas ruled that, because the
state legislature had to pass a special law putting the colonists
in possession of their land, the original act of 1842 was nul-
lified. Therefore the colonists were under no legal obligation
to pay Castro one-half of their granted lands. Thus the court
settled the last major question on the distribution of Castro
colony land.[29]

Between 1842, when Castro received his grant, and 1855,
when the last of the property was distributed, the empresario
transported over 2,000 immigrants to Texas, founded four
towns, and instituted the first major settlement west of San
Antonio. He pursued the single-minded course of establishing the grant. He became the only individual during the
republic period in Texas who followed his empresario contract through to a successful completion. All the others either
sold out or included some large group to complete their
obligations.

Castro, like many land promoters, displayed a curious
combination of romanticism and hard-headed business acumen. He envisioned a sort of personal kingdom in Texas
where he would be the great landholder and all the colonists
would be beholden to him for bringing them to their new
landholder position. To accomplish his ends the man relied
upon an easy conscience and a glib tongue to carry him to
success. He nearly achieved his aim. In terms of land holdings he was successful. Only the nearly worthless value of the

[28]"Humbug Property," Haass Papers, Texas Collection; Survey of deed records in the seven counties constituting Castro's Colony for property holdings of
Henry Castro, which were compared to lands auctioned off by Illis to give the
amount of land left in the possession of Castro.
[29]Angelo Causici vs. J. B. LaCosta and Albert Huth, Statement of Facts, January 16, 1857, Bexar County Archives.

property within the grant prevented him from accomplishing his ultimate goal.

The land wealth presented by Castro colony lands did not long remain in the hands of the colonists. Castro secured the lion's share of slightly over 50 percent of the property while speculators got another 25 percent. The colonists remained on their smaller plots near the villages they founded. The colonists living on the grant had to be satisfied with their new life because they had little choice in the matter. Castro, particularly after the Illis lawsuit, was not wealthy, but he had a comfortable life. By 1855 the land was distributed and all the participants settled down to a stable existence.

CHAPTER VIII

Settling In: 1850–65

By 1855 the Castro colonists who would acquire their land had received it. Those colonists who were not involved in land distribution had scattered among the towns that lined the long winding road from the coast, returned to Europe, or more likely succumbed to the perils of the frontier land that was Texas. It was time for them to settle into their new life, which the local situation, combined with national events, strongly influenced. Geographic conditions forced them into stock raising. Many of the colonists became more politically active as a result of the anti-immigrant Know-Nothing movement. They opposed the Southern approach to secession and were Union supporters during the Civil War. By 1865 the colony had emerged as a region with a distinctive European flavor, but with a much greater involvement in American social, economic, and political life.

The decade between 1850 and 1860 proved to be a time of change for the colonists. During that period the regional geographic conditions forced the colonists to adapt to their new environment. This is perhaps best illustrated by the occupations of the colonists. In 1850 their declared occupations ranged from farmer to hotelkeeper, but the greatest number of persons listed such trades as mason, wheelwright, carpenter, shoemaker, or watchmaker, while a minority claimed to be farmers. In the 1850 census Medina County contained 177 heads of households of whom 69 or 39.9 percent were farmers. By 1860 heads of households living in the area numbered 362 of whom 255 or 70 percent claimed to be farmers. Of the 39 heads of households who could be traced from 1850 through 1860, 17 indicated they were farmers in 1850 while in 1860 31 counted themselves farmers. This change in occupational status probably represents more of a change in attitude than a radical occupational shift. The primary work available to the colonists, both in 1850 and 1860, was farming. Texas, and particularly a frontier area like Castro's colony, simply could not support the kinds of occupations listed in the 1850 census. In 1850 the colonists who had so recently arrived from their European homelands still thought of themselves in terms of their European occupations. In the ensuing ten years they became accustomed enough to their new homeland and life-style to think of themselves as farmers.[1]

Another important change in occupation related to the geographic location of the colony. The 1850 census listed only one stock raiser in the colony area. By 1860 23 were listed, a change that indicated an adaptation to geographic realities of life in a region less suitable for agriculture than for ranching. Perhaps Simon Fest best characterized the change to this life-style. He arrived in Texas aboard the *Schanunga* in 1846, proceeded to the colony, and began trying to farm. Unable to survive financially, he moved to San Antonio where he plied his old trade of stonemason. Often receiving payment for his work in cattle, Simon eventually moved to the outskirts of town to provide grazing land for his growing herd. In 1852, after selling his granted 640 acres in the colony to Castro, he bought land on the Gallinas River south of San Antonio where he ranched until his death in 1859. The family later transferred its herd to the Pleasanton region where they established a ranch that a son, Henry, operated during and after the Civil War.[2]

The Wantz family illustrates the typical pattern of those

[1] U.S. Seventh Census (1850), Schedule I: Free Inhabitants, Medina County; U.S. Eighth Census (1860), Schedule I: Free Inhabitants, Medina County.

[2] U.S. Seventh Census (1850), Schedule I: Free Inhabitants, and Schedule III: Agriculture, Medina County; Ship's List for the *Schanunga*, Colonization Papers; Archives, Texas State Library, Austin; John Marvin Hunter, *The Trail Drivers of Texas*, I: 459; Castro Colony Land Certificate Book, H. E. Haass, Papers, Barker Texas History Center, University of Texas, Austin; Deed Records, Medina County, County Clerk's Office, Hondo.

who remained on the grant. They arrived early in 1845 aboard the *Probus* and by 1850 had settled at Vandenburg. The father, Ignatz, an energetic farmer from Bas Rhin, soon saw the advantages of cattle raising in conjunction with farming. He died in 1859, but by the time of the Civil War the Wantz family had accumulated a sizable herd. Unfortunately, during the course of the war the family lost most of its livestock while male members were away fighting and the women who stayed home were unable to care for the herd. After the conflict Xavier Wantz, the youngest son, built the cattle operation into a prosperous medium-size enterprise.[3]

Population change augmented this adaptation to the geographical demands of the area. After 1850 a new wave of settlement took place in Medina County. The native Anglos from the eastern part of Texas began to move into the county. They tended to settle west and south of the Castro settlements where they engaged primarily in cattle and sheep ranching. But more important to the colony were the large numbers of German immigrants who settled in its midst. Some had heard of the colony through friends or relatives among the original colonists but arrived too late to get land. Others were simply immigrants looking for people of a similar cultural background for neighbors. They came from the German states for the most part and were not considered Alsatian.[4]

The Rothe family provides a good example of those new German immigrants. The father, Henry, brought his family from Bavaria to Castroville in 1854 to join relatives already settled in the colony. Although shocked by the death of Henry's wife on the trip from the coast to Castroville, the family continued on to settle near the Medina River above Castroville. They entered the cattle business almost immediately. When unable to get free land, they began to herd livestock in return for a percentage of the increase. With the

---

[3] Ship's List for *Probus*, Colonization Papers; U.S. Seventh Census (1850), Schedule I: Free Inhabitants, Medina County; Hunter, *Trail Drivers*, II: 719–20.

[4] This information was derived by taking the U.S. Eighth Census (1860), Schedule I: Free Inhabitants for Medina County and by using the child-ladder method determine the arrival date and place of origin of the inhabitants.

outbreak of the Civil War the two older Rothe brothers went off to fight, leaving the two younger brothers to look after their growing herd. Having someone to care for the cattle during the war allowed them to increase their holdings so that by the 1870s and 1880s the brothers—August, Henry, Fritz, and Louis—owned more than 100,000 acres and leased enough additional land to run 16,000 head of livestock. The Rothes achieved spectacular success, but their beginnings in the mid-1850s were typical of other families in the area, one noted for successful livestock business.[5]

Many of the German immigrants arrived in Medina County in the 1850s for reasons other than the desire for land that had motivated most of the original settlers. Some of them had fled the political unrest engendered by the 1848 revolutions in Europe. Notable among these immigrants was H. J. Richarz, who arrived in 1849 after taking an active part in the revolutions. He became a pioneer sheep raiser in Texas, starting a 500-acre sheep ranch near San Antonio shortly after his arrival. Using several Saxony rams he brought from Germany, he quickly gained a reputation as an innovator by breeding his rams with the poor grade of Mexican sheep to produce a commercially profitable product. In 1853 he moved to Dhanis where he established a ranch, raising both cattle and sheep. By 1854 his sheep operation consisted of 300 good sheep produced by breeding the Saxony rams to Mexican ewes. Richarz also provided shelter and hay for his animals during the winter, a typical European practice not used by the Anglo ranchers in the area, who lost large numbers of their sheep to exposure, in contrast to Richarz's negligible losses.[6]

As environmental influences combined with new immigration to create a changing economic focus in the colony, the colonists also tried to cope with political change. Upon the founding of Castroville in 1844 Castro guided the election of

[5] Myrtle Murray, "Home Life on Early Ranches in Southwest Texas," *Cattleman,* August, 1938, 19; Andrew Jackson Sowell, *Early Settlers and Indian Fighters of Southwest Texas,* 233, 240; John Marvin Hunter, *One Hundred Years in Bandera, 1853–1953,* 14; Frederick Law Olmsted, *A Journey Through Texas,* 280–81.

[6] Sowell, *Settlers,* 202; Olmsted, *Journey,* 259.

G. L. Haass as constable and of Louis Huth and J. S. Bourgeois as justices of the peace. At that time the region was still a part of Bexar County, thus the elected Castroville officials served the county. Castro carefully observed the details of legality in the elections of men who supported him, thus building a legal base to maintain order and control over the colony.

By 1848 the settled area of the colony contained a sufficiently large population to seek organization as a county. That year the state government created and organized Medina County with Castroville as the county seat. "The founder of the Colony, Henry Castro," drafted the petition seeking county status for an area embracing the colony villages of Castroville, Quihi, Vandenburg, and Dhanis. It claimed that 1,000 people lived within the bounds of the colony and the petition contained the signatures of 67 persons, all of whom were certified as members of the colony.[7]

From the time of the formal organization of the county in 1848 neither Castro nor any member of his family held elected public office. His grandson, Angelo Causici, was appointed notary public in 1848 and held that post until at least the beginning of the Civil War, while his son, Lorenzo Castro, was appointed notary public for August 1856 until July 1857. At the same time Louis Huth, whom Castro considered an enemy, won election as tax assessor in 1848, county clerk from 1850 through 1858, and chief justice from 1860 through 1862. Original colonists held all other elective offices in the county from 1848 until 1852, when an increasing number of newcomers began to be elected to key positions. Thus during the decade of the 1850s Henry Castro lost control over the colonists he had brought from Europe. The large number of enemies he made among the colonists with his land speculation cost him any political power he might have retained within the area of the colony.[8]

    [7] Henri Castro, Journal, Henri Castro Papers, Barker Texas History Center, University of Texas at Austin; Walter Prescott Webb, ed., *Handbook of Texas*, II: 168; Petition to establish Medina County, January 6, 1848, Memorials and Petitions, Archives, Texas State Library, Austin.
    [8] Election Register 258: 158–59, Election Register 259: 328–29, Texas, Secretary of State Records, Archives, Texas State Library, Austin; Lt. Col. A. G. Dickinson

As the empresario lost control over his colonists and consolidated ownership over as much of the granted land as possible, he tried to expand his economic interests in other areas. In 1850 he started a general mercantile store in Eagle Pass, Texas, but unfortunately a fire destroyed his building and entire stock of goods. This affair ended with a lawsuit that resulted in a $20,000 judgment against Castro. Meanwhile, the empresario maintained an income through acting as landlord over much of the farmland he owned in the out-lot area east of the Medina River and through sale of the property he acquired from the grant.[9]

The erosion of Castro's influence over the colony, the growing importance of livestock raising in the area, and the formalization of local political activity developed as logical adaptations of the immigrant population to its new environment. But this activity was played out against the much larger panorama of national events. Castro's colony developed during the period when Texas gave up its independence to become a state within the United States. Much of the immigration occurred between 1846 and 1848 while the Mexican War was being fought. Many of the younger immigrants entered the war as soldiers before they even saw the land they came to settle. Their military experience during this time prepared them for the frontier existence they faced on the grant. It also exposed them to an intensive contact with American social and political activities not available on the grant. After the war, when the land question was being settled, the veterans along with the rest of the colonists found themselves gradually drawn into the national political situation.[10]

By 1854 an anti-Catholic and anti-immigrant movement manifested in the American or Know-Nothing Party became a major national political reality. Texas had its share of strong

---

to Capt. E. P. Turner, October 12, 1863, in *The War of the Rebellion: A Compilation of the Official Records of the Union and Confederate Armies*, Series I, Vol. XLVIII, Pt. II, 899–900, cited hereafter as *Official Records*.

[9] Jno. W. Whitlock vs. Henry Castro, April 30, 1852, John W. Whitlock and Co. vs. Henry Castro, October 20, 1852, Jno. W. Whitlock vs. Henry Castro, May 3, 1853, Bexar County Archives, Bexar County Courthouse, San Antonio; August Santleben, *A Texas Pioneer*, 6–7.

[10] Sowell, *Settlers*, 202–203, 347–49, 542–44, 556–60.

Know-Nothing supporters who called for exclusion of immigrants from holding public office while at the same time recommending a longer time period before immigrants could gain citizenship. The German community in Texas banded together in solid opposition to the threat. On July 23, 1855, German-Americans held a mass meeting in San Antonio opposing the Know-Nothings and supporting the Democratic Party. Their list of nine resolutions strongly denounced the nativistic attack on loyal American citizens. Only two days earlier the citizens of Castroville had held a similar meeting, which adopted resolutions for Louis Huth to present at the San Antonio gathering. The Castro colony resolutions, while stronger than those of the larger San Antonio conclave, accurately portrayed the colonists' attitudes toward their new homeland.

Whereas, religious bigots and old effete brokendown politicians have formed a secret organization, with the avowed purpose of disenfranchising a large portion of the citizens of this glorious Republic. Therefore, be it resolved, that we will support no man for the office, at the coming election, who is not uncompromisingly opposed to the Anti-American conspiracy, commonly termed the Know Nothing party. Resolved, that the doctrines of religious intolerance and proscription promulgated by the anti-American or Know Nothings, are a disgrace to the age in which we live.
Resolved, that we consider it our duty, as well as the duty of every American, to maintain to the last extremity the equal and inalienable rights of all our citizens, as at present guaranteed to us by the Constitution of the United States.

The colonists then endorsed E. M. Pease for governor, P. H. Bell for Congress, Samuel Maverick for senator, and Jacob Waelder for representative. That slate of candidates gained overwhelming support in the 1855 elections.[11]

The Know-Nothing movement represented a direct threat that drew the newly arrived colonists together in common cause against an easily perceived enemy. After the 1855 elections the Know-Nothing problem faded from the scene,

[11] Austin *Texas State Gazette*, August 1, 1855; E. W. Winkler, *Platforms of Political Parties in Texas*, 68–71.

but the problem of the larger North-South sectional conflict replaced that narrow nativistic threat.

During the 1850s the Texas population grew rapidly, primarily because of people migrating from other Southern states. They brought with them Southern attitudes toward economic and social activities. During this decade the numbers of slaves and slaveowners in the state increased dramatically. Medina County did not fit this general pattern of development. The population of the county consisted almost exclusively of an immigrant group operating subsistence farms and engaging in the embryonic ranching business. In 1850 there were only 22 slaves in the colony area, owned by a total of 8 persons. But by 1860 the numbers had increased to 106 slaves owned by 22 individuals as traditional Southern Anglos entered the region in increasing numbers. Even with that increase the area showed little evidence of significant economic control by the slaveowners, while the local political leaders reflected the character of the hardworking and frugal European settlers they represented.[12]

The Medina County folk apparently did not become actively involved in either side of the North-South debate as the national election of 1860 neared. Meanwhile, during the spring and summer of 1860 national politics reached a boiling point as the Democratic Party split into two factions. The national party nominated Stephen Douglas of Illinois for president. This alienated the radical Southern faction of the party, which broke away and nominated John C. Breckinridge of Kentucky as its candidate. Then to complicate matters further another group composed of former Whigs and former Know-Nothing supporters nominated John Bell of Tennessee. These disarrayed parties faced a united Republican Party whose candidate was Abraham Lincoln of Illinois.

[12] The most detailed discussion of the development of southern slaveowners' control in Texas may be found in Joe T. Timmons, "Texas on the Road to Secession" (Ph.D. dissertation, University of Chicago, 1973); U.S. Seventh Census (1850), Medina County, Texas, Schedule I: Population, Schedule II: Slaves, and Schedule III: Agriculture; U.S. Eighth Census (1860), Schedule I: Population, Schedule II: Slaves, and Schedule IV: Agriculture; Election Register 258: 158–59, and Election Register 259: 328–29, Texas, Secretary of State Records, Archives, Texas State Library, Austin.

On November 6, 1860, the name of Lincoln did not even appear on the ballot in the presidential election in Texas, and Douglas received only a few votes. Texans cast 63,947 votes of which Breckinridge received 76 percent or 48,376. In Medina County, Breckinridge received 148 of 189 votes cast or a 78 percent majority, with only 45 percent of the electorate voting. The small voter turnout indicated a decided lack of interest when the choice lay between a radical Southern candidate and one who represented the Know-Nothing threat the colonists only recently had protested.[13]

Many Texas political leaders took Lincoln's election victory as a mandate for action and called a secession convention. The Castro colony area sent as delegates to the convention A. Nauendorf, a well-to-do German merchant from San Antonio who owned no slaves, and Charles DeMontel, who had been with the colonists from the beginning and had amassed a considerable estate in addition to owning seven slaves. The Ordinance of Secession was adopted by the convention by a vote of 166 to 8 with both Medina County delegates voting in favor.[14]

When the ordinance went to the voters of the state on February 23, 1861, they chose to secede by a vote of 46,188 of 61,008 ballots cast, or 76 percent of the total. Medina County had a voter turnout of 347, which represented 83 percent of the electorate. The county went against state sentiment when 60 percent of the voters, or 207 out of 347, cast ballots against secession. Many of the Castro colonists, who had felt little motivation to vote in 1860, suddenly found themselves facing a very serious question in 1861. Going to the polls in large numbers, they chose not to support secession and the possible war that might follow.[15]

[13] Bruce Catton, *The Coming Fury*, 1–235; Austin *Texas State Gazette*, November 17, 1860; Walter Dean Burnham, *Presidential Ballots, 1836–1892*, 794–95; the estimate of 45% of the eligible voters was arrived at by counting all free white males over the age of twenty-one years in the 1860 Medina County Census (the number of eligible voters came to 420).
[14] Ralph A. Wooster, "An Analysis of the Membership of the Texas Secession Convention," *Southwestern Historical Quarterly* 70 (January, 1967): 328–32.
[15] Ernest W. Winkler, ed., *Journal of the Secession Convention of Texas, 1861*, 88–90; Secession Election Returns, Medina County, Archives, Texas State Library.

Even before war began, the colonists became involved in seizing control of the frontier forts in Texas. On February 21, 1861, James Paul of Castroville received a commission from representatives acting on behalf of the Committee of Public Safety of the State of Texas to raise a company of Texas Mounted Rangers. He enrolled twenty-six men, eighteen of whom were colonists, and marched to Camp Verde on Verde Creek several miles above Castroville. The camp, which had served as a U.S. military post since 1857, contained a garrison of Union troops. Paul's force arrived at the post on March 6 and after a long session of negotiation allowed the Union troops to leave the following day in possession of all their arms, ammunition, and horses. The little military force then occupied the fort including "the stores, ammunition, twelve mules, eighty camels, and two Egyptian drivers." On May 16 the ranger company disbanded and the post remained deserted for the duration of the war.[16]

Along with this first bloodless military action other activities in Medina County indicated support for the Confederate cause. By early June the Committee of Safety for Medina County formed. This organization sought to preserve order in the county and support the Confederate cause until more formal political institutions could be formed. Its thirty-four members, of whom only fifteen were colonists, swore an oath of secrecy concerning their activities, which included a martial-law trial for lawbreakers brought before them.[17]

Yet another manifestation of Southern sympathy during 1861 appeared with the formation of a Knights of the Golden Circle castle at Castroville. This secret organization, which developed in the years just prior to the Civil War, tried to promote the interests of the slave-owning South. The membership of the Castroville castle numbered thirty-eight, of whom all but four were colonists. James Paul served as a lead-

[16]Muster Roll of 1st Lieut. James Paul's Company of Texas Mounted Rangers, March 4, 1861, Archives, Texas State Library; R. H. Williams, *With the Border Ruffians*, 164–67; Muster Roll, March 4, 1861; Payroll no. 72, 1st Lieut. James A. Paul's Company of Texas Rangers, May 16, 1861, Archives, Texas State Library.

[17]Constitution of the "Committee of Public Safety" of Medina County, Castroville File, James Menke Collection, San Antonio.

ing figure in both the Committee of Safety and the Knights
of the Golden Circle in addition to being the commander of
the force that captured Camp Verde. It is not clear why the
immigrants supported such an organization, but the dynamic personality of Paul evidently persuaded them to become actively involved in the new regime in its first months.[18]

The sympathy shown the Southern cause by the colonists in early 1861 did not last long nor did it extend to the
majority of the Medina County residents. Most of the colonists eligible to enter the army enlisted in frontier regiments
organized from the counties bordering on the northern and
western edges of Texas. These men could serve and not leave
their homes while at the same time providing protection
for their homes and families from Indian raids and the unlikely possibility of Union military incursion.[19]

By 1863 the colonists obviously used this means to avoid
serving in the Confederate Army. In May of that year two
companies of Confederate cavalry moved into Medina County
to arrest conscripts not deemed necessary for defense against
Indian attack. The soldiers arrested twenty-five men, but another twenty were warned and managed to escape. The
officer in charge of the operation recommended that "If
martial law was proclaimed in Medina County and other
counties adjoining, I think the disaffected could be brought
to punishment."[20]

The view of the military received support through a
letter from several Medina County citizens who complained
about the unionist sentiment in the county. The signers of
the letter, including Franck Riecherger, Charles DeMontel,

[18] Roy Sylvan Dunn, "The KGB in Texas, 1860–1861," *Southwestern Historical Quarterly* 70 (April, 1967), 543–73; Bylaws of the Castroville Castle "KGB," Approved August 16, 1861, Castroville File, Menke Collection.

[19] *Military Law of Texas, An Act to Perfect the Organization of the State Troops,* 3–4; Muster Roll, Capt. George Mayer, Medina County, 31st Brigade, Texas State Troops, August, 1862; Muster Roll, Lieut. Saathof Focke, Texas State Troops, 31st Militia Brigade, October 6, 1863; Muster Roll, Lieut. F. Haby, Medina County, 31st Brigade, October 23, 1863; Muster Roll, Lieut. Augustine Weber, Castroville, Medina County, 3rd Frontier District, March 1864; Muster Roll, Capt. George Robbins, Frontier Company, March 7, 1864, Archives, Texas State Library.

[20] Smith P. Bankhead to Capt. Edmund P. Turner, May 20, 1863, *Official Records,* XLVIII, Pt. II, 13.

Thomas P. Wycale and G. S. Haass, who all held political positions with the Confederacy, stated that "a majority of the citizens of Medina County are disloyal toward the Confederate States." Additionally they charged that most of the elected officials in Medina County sympathized with the disloyal population. They even claimed that the officials distributed funds meant for dependent families of Confederate soldiers to the families of deserters and traitors.[21]

Meanwhile, most of the colonists had left Texas and gone to Mexico to escape serving the Confederacy. Others, like Lorenzo Castro, who became customs collector at Eagle Pass on the Mexican border, assumed various official posts to escape serving in the army. Even Henri Castro, nearly eighty at the time, attempted to gain a similar position. Many of the able-bodied men who fled Medina County to Mexico joined the First Texas Cavalry Regiment of the Union Army. They served in that unit until the end of the war when they returned home to resume the life they had intended when they came to Texas.[22]

As for Henri Castro, after his unsuccessful attempt at gaining government employment he evidently became involved in business activities in Mexico. He died at Monterrey, Mexico on November 3, 1863, and was buried there. Tradition suggests that his death occurred during an attempt to return to France to visit relatives, but it is more likely that he was on some business errand to recoup some of his lost fortune.[23]

The position of the Castro colonists during the Civil War was a shattering experience that came just as they were cementing their situation on the grant. When the colonists voted against secession and later opposed the war and even

[21] Ibid., 13–14.

[22] Lieut. Col. A. G. Dickinson to Capt. E. P. Turner, October 12, 1863, *Official Records*, XLVIII, Pt. II, 899–900; Jesse Sumpter, "Life of Jesse Sumpter, the Oldest Living Citizen of Eagle Pass, Texas (1902)," Barker Texas History Center, University of Texas at Austin; Lorenzo Castro to Denis Conger, December 15, 1862, Confederate Records, Record Group 365, National Archives, Washington, D.C.; *Report of the Adjutant General of the State of Texas, June 24, 1870, to December 31, 1870, Appendix*, 4–40.

[23] Ruth Curry Lawler, *The Story of Castroville*, 27.

joined Union forces, their different background came into sharp focus. They were adamant that their life go on as planned, which did not include fighting a war against the nation that had been furnishing troops that had helped them with protection of life and property. That factor of a stable government including military protection was probably the most important reason for the colonists' support of the Union cause.

The problem of frontier defense was a major element of the colonists' existence beginning with Castro's 1842 contract. The republic originally viewed the colony as a frontier buffer against military threats to Texas from the west. The fortune in land that the empresario promised the colonists became the primary incentive that drew them to the grant. This same incentive drove Castro to organize an effective colonization recruiting and transport program whose most important element, other than the dynamic personality of the empresario, was the solid work of the Huth family. But even with Louis Huth in Texas directing activities the exposed frontier position of the colony prevented effective settlement. From the outset of the project frontier protection had played a pivotal part in the operation.

When Castro established Castroville in 1844, he provided a substantial base that offered protection to the colonists. Yet the first settlement west of Castroville, Quihi, suffered a disastrous Indian attack just as it was founded. This event, plus the sporadic protection offered by Republic of Texas forces, left the settlements largely unprotected. Finally the U.S. military brought effective protection when they established Fort Lincoln after the Mexican War.

The idea of a stable government to protect life and property focused on property as much as it did on life. After all, acquisition of property was the primary purpose of the entire colonization project. The Republic of Texas planned to pay for frontier protection with land. Accordingly, Castro and the colonists desired the land as a source of wealth. That idea kept the empresario working against all odds until he achieved his goal. His various financial dealings in Europe and Texas, including the deal with the Belgian businessmen, were often unethical, but they always had as their goal the successful completion of the colonization project.

The colonists Castro brought to Texas formed a distinctive culture in the area of their settlement. They introduced a distinctive architecture, established a Catholic center on the frontier, and served their purpose as a frontier military buffer zone. By the time their land was distributed most of them preferred to live on and farm the small plots of land Castro distributed to them in the relatively fertile parts of the grant rather than use the grant land proper. Thus Castro received the greatest amount of the grant property, which, because of its limited value netted him only a modest income. Nevertheless, the empresario carried his project to a successful conclusion through his stubborn refusal to abandon it despite almost insurmountable odds.

The success of Castro's colony did not take place in a vacuum. While he was settling his grant, another successful colonization was developing. The Peters colony in North Texas settled 5,386 persons on its gigantic preserve. The Peters colony settlers were recruited primarily from the Ohio Valley and represented a small farm-owning population.[24]

Although the Peters colony had no close ties to Castro's colony the Society for the Protection of German Immigrants in Texas was closely linked with the Castro operation. The empresario considered the Adelsverein, as it was usually called, his competition. This was particularly true after the organization bought the Fisher-Miller grant in 1844. The two organizations competed ferociously for colonists to settle their grants. Despite the competition, however, when neither organization could muster enough colonists to fill a particular immigrant ship, the two groups many times cooperatively chartered vessels to Texas. This cooperation was always temporary, however, and there is no evidence that either group voluntarily allowed colonists from one organization to move to the other's settlements.[25]

The Adelsverein was organized by a group of German

[24] Seymour V. Connor, *The Peters Colony of Texas*, 94–120.
[25] Ships' Lists, Colonization Papers.

noblemen who had tremendous influence in Germany. Their activities no doubt reduced the effectiveness of Castro's recruitment with Germany. The German group brought 7,380 Germans to Texas which, combined with the 2,134 introduced by Castro, put a total of almost 10,000 Europeans in Texas by their combined efforts. These 10,000 Europeans were scattered along the western edge of the Texas frontier while the 5,000 Peters colony settlers guarded the northern frontier. The combination of these 15,000 settlers did much to protect the interior of Texas from Indian depredations in the 1840s and 1850s.[26]

The differences between the pattern of settlement of the Anglo settlers of the Peters colony and the European settlers was considerable. To the north the Anglos settled in traditional American isolated farmsteads. But the Europeans, whose pattern of settlement resulted largely from Castro's activities, settled in villages. Castro's first contingent arrived in January of 1843, well over a year before the Adelsverein's first ship. When Castro put his colonists on town lots and provided them with twenty- and forty-acre farm plots in September of 1844, he developed an excellent system for introducing the immigrants to their new environment. Solms-Braunfels followed Castro's example in March 1845 when he bought land and established the town of New Braunfels some thirty miles northeast of San Antonio. Prince Carl also put his settlers on town lots and provided them with tiny ten-acre plots until arrangements could be made to occupy the land granted to the settlers.[27]

Few of the European colonists were able to settle on their granted property due to its poor quality and the danger from Indian attack. The larger numbers of the Germans allowed them to form the towns of New Braunfels in 1845 and Fredericksburg in 1846. Both of these towns had larger popu-

[26]Rudolph Leopold Biesele, *The History of German Settlements in Texas*, 66–82; John O. Muesbach, *Answer to Interrogatories*, 16; Henri Castro, *Memorial of Henry Castro, Founder of Castro's Colony to the Senate and the House of Representatives of the State of Texas*.

[27]Connor, *Peters Colony*, 94–120; Castro, Journal; Biesele, *German Settlements*, 118–21.

lations than Castroville or any other of the three Castro settlements, but neither town was on the Fisher-Miller grant. By contrast the Peters-colony people settled directly on their granted property, which was in a fertile section of Texas.[28]

When it came time for the settlers to receive title to their property, they all experienced problems. Litigation over the Peters property dragged on into the 1870s before the last of the lands were distributed, and none of the leaders of the project realized a profit. The Adelsverein greatly underestimated the expense of founding its colony and abdicated its financial responsibilities when it turned over all its assets to creditors in 1847. The towns of New Braunfels and Fredericksburg continued to flourish as centers of attraction for German immigration to western Texas up until the Civil War and afterward. By contrast Castro managed to settle his entire land question by 1855, although not to the complete satisfaction of all participants.[29]

The types of settlers attracted to the various colonies varied somewhat. The Peters colony had a rather homogeneous group of colonists who originated largely in the Ohio River Valley and were almost entirely Protestant. The Adelsverein settlement area was also very homogeneous and was characterized by being entirely German and overwhelmingly Protestant with a tiny Catholic minority. Castro's colonists represented a much more cosmopolitan population composed largely of Alsatians but with representatives of a large number of European nationalities in their midst. They were Catholic for the most part with a small group of Lutherans in certain localities. These particular groupings of nationality and religion still dominate the areas of colony settlement.[30]

Perhaps the most common element to the three colony areas in the 1850s was that all opposed secession. Slaves were

[28] By mid-1847 the town of New Braunfels had an estimated population of between 1,500 and 2,000 inhabitants. See Biesele, *German Settlements*, 132, 145; Connor, *Peters Colony*, 94–120.

[29] Connor, *Peters Colony*, 120; Biesele, *German Settlements*, 159–60.

[30] Connor, *Peters Colony*, 94–120; Biesele, *German Settlements*, 135, 143–44; Parish Register, St. Louis Catholic Church, Castroville, Texas; U.S. Seventh Census (1850), Schedule I: Free Inhabitants, Medina County; U.S. Eighth Census (1860), Schedule I: Free Inhabitants, Medina County; Ships' Lists, Colonization Papers.

a scarce commodity in all the colony areas. All of them voted against secession and all of them experienced difficulties during the Civil War because of their unionist attitudes.

The efforts of the various empresario projects under the auspices of the Republic of Texas produced long-range results. Henri Castro established the first successful European colony under that authority. His dogged determination, which produced that result, involved large-scale European advertisement concerning the advantages of living in Texas. The work of Castro and his chief competitor, the Adelsverein, as well as the Peters colony organization resulted in a continually expanding pre–Civil War European and Ohio Valley immigration to Texas.[31] This immigration increased the population, brought much-needed skills and finances, and vastly enriched cultural heritage of the Lone Star State.

---

[31] Ethel Hander Geue, *New Homes in a New Land*, 31–37; Connor, *Peters Colony*, 164.

Bibliography

Note on Sources

Much of the source material for this work on Castro's colony is applicable to any study on European immigration to Texas. This discussion will point the serious researcher toward major resources that provide answers to questions of official government stance on immigration, statistical data on arrivals, land acquisition, and adaptation to life in Texas.

A few sources must be used in writing about immigration to the Republic of Texas, and particularly emigration from Europe. George P. Garrison's *Diplomatic Correspondence of the Republic of Texas*, Ephraim Douglass Adam's *British Diplomatic Correspondence Concerning the Republic of Texas*, and Nancy Nichols Barker's *The French Legation in Texas*, are essential edited works that provide government correspondence. This material provides the official stance of the government plus a wealth of insight into the character of specific individuals. *The Writings of Sam Houston* by Amelia W. Williams and Eugene C. Barker supplies similar information.

Originally, the ships' lists of Castro's and all other empresario projects were filed with Texas officials. These lists, along with any official correspondence relating to the various Republic of Texas colonization attempts, are organized under the heading of Colonization Papers at the Archives Division of the Texas State Library at Austin. This group of records, combined with the published official correspondence, provides the most complete record of the activities of European immigration to Texas during the republic period. Approximately three quarters of the Colonization Papers are English, but many of the records are in French and German.

One direct result of European settlement in Texas was the permanent establishment of religious bodies, particularly Catholic and Lutheran organizations. The records of these bodies, whose representatives were closely involved with the immigrants, contain much valuable data. The various Catholic diocese archives, Lutheran church records, and Catholic church records contain a variety of statistical information, official letters, and reminiscences. The most important of these is the Catholic Archives of Texas at Austin. This repository contains the most complete collection of Bishop Jean Marie Odin's correspondence as well as collections from various churches and individuals from throughout the state. Despite a monumental effort to acquire all Catholic historical records pertaining to Texas, the Catholic Archives of Texas has only a portion of those records in its files. Next in importance to this archive, for Republic of Texas material, is the Archive of the Diocese of Galveston-Houston at Houston. Approximately three-quarters of Catholic correspondence in the state is in French, German, Italian, or Latin. For example, Bishop Odin's letters are almost without exception in French.

An important source for researching land holdings as well as specific individuals' activities is the General Land Office of Texas located in Austin. This state agency was established during the first days of the republic to maintain the official records of all public lands and maintains a file on the original ownership of every parcel of land in the state. These files, which often contain considerable correspondence pertaining to a particular transaction, can be accessed by a computerized printout, alphabetized according to the last name of the person who filed the original application for the land. The agency also has all the original Spanish records pertaining to Texas lands as well as the original land records of the various empresarios involved in settlement, both under Mexican and republic auspices. The map division of the General Land Office maintains a variety of historic maps in addition to original land-ownership maps for each county in the state. The increasing need to better organize the historic holdings of this active state agency has prompted the establishment of its archive division in January of 1984 to better serve the historical research community of Texas.

The research in General Land Office records must be coordinated with research in county government records to determine the ultimate disposition of property beyond original ownership. For Castro's colony, the use of deed records, wills, and lawsuits found in various county courthouses clarified what happened to colony land after it was given to the grantee. This activity requires considerable effort in the county clerk's office of specific counties and requires care in being aware of the changing physical configuration of the county over time. Although records for newly formed counties were supposed to be transferred to the new entities at the time of formation, this activity was not always strictly observed. Therefore many historically significant items are not reposited in the present courthouses that have jurisdiction over the area where the event transpired.

The material pertaining specifically to Castro's colony comes from a variety of places. Four major collections provide the bulk of archival information. The largest of these is the Ferdinand Louis Huth Papers at the Barker Texas History Center at the University of Texas at Austin. The Huth letters were written, for the most part, by Ludwig Huth in Baden to his son Ferdinand Louis in Texas between 1842 and 1848. Although they are primarily concerned with colony affairs, they contain considerable information on conditions in Europe as well as European perceptions of Texas. The Huth correspondence is all in German with a few French phrases; approximately half has been translated, and the rest is slated for translation soon. The second collection is the Henri Castro Papers, also at the Barker Center. The Castro Papers consist of copies of material Castro had in his possession including his journal, "Le Texas" (a recruiting pamphlet), "Le Emprunt" by Jacques Lafitte (an essay on the $5 million loan), and various pieces of correspondence relating to the colony. Most of the material in the Castro Papers is in French. The other two collections both originated with H. E. Haass and are known as the H. E. Haass Papers—one of them is located in the Barker Texas History Center and the other in the Texas Collection at Baylor University. The Haass Papers consist of a variety of miscellaneous materials pertaining to Castro's colony and Medina County. Perhaps the most valuable single item in this collection is a copy of the Castro Colony Land Certificate book, the original of which has since been lost from the General Land Office of Texas.

Occasionally private collections provide valuable assistance to historical researchers. James Menke of San Antonio has provided that service for Castro's colony. Several years ago he started collecting material on Medina County. His collection, primarily organized by family name for genealogical research, is a treasure trove of historical data. Beyond the family reminiscences that make up the bulk of the data, it contains ships' lists, Medina County and Castroville official records, church data, and a myriad of details relating to activities in the region. Menke's years of gleaning information from the descendants of Castro colonists provides the data base for creating a synthesis of the colonists' life-style.

To summarize, major research sources for a study of this kind include several sources. The Barker Texas History Center at the University of Texas and the Archives Division of the Texas State Library collectively contain the most comprehensive body of records. The General Land Office of Texas in Austin and specific county courthouses used together will provide most answers on land questions. Church-related archives and private collections round out the information available from original sources. Beyond these, checking the smaller archives around the state, using census records, and making a standard bibliographic search of secondary sources, newspapers, journals, and published documents will complete basic research on immigration to the Republic of Texas.

Primary Material

Documents

Bexar County Archives. Bexar County Courthouse, San Antonio.

Blevins Papers. Witte Museum Library, San Antonio.

Brucks, A. B. "History of New Fountain Church." New Fountain File, James Menke Collection, San Antonio.

Butterfield, Jack C. "The Free State of Bejar." Daughters of the Republic of Texas Library, San Antonio.

Castro, Henri. Journal. Henri Castro Papers, Barker Texas History Center, University of Texas at Austin.

———. "Le Texas." H. E. Haass Papers, Texas Collection, Baylor University, Waco.

———. "Le Texas." Henri Castro Papers, Barker Texas History Center, University of Texas at Austin.

Castroville File. James Menke Collection, San Antonio.

Castroville Papers. Catholic Archives of Texas, Austin.

Church Records. Bethlehem Luthern Church, Quihi.

Church Records. Zion Lutheran Church, Castroville.

Colonization Papers. Archives, Texas State Library, Austin.

Customs Office Records, Confederate States, Department of the Treasury, Eagle Pass District, Texas. National Archives of the United States, Washington, D.C.

Dashiell, Jeremiah Jellot. Correspondence. Barker Texas History Center, University of Texas at Austin.

Deed Records. County Clerk's Office, Atascosa County, Jourdantan.
———. County Clerk's Office, Bexar County, San Antonio.
———. County Clerk's Office, Frio County, Pearsall.
———. County Clerk's Office, La Salle County, Cotulla.
———. County Clerk's Office, McMullen County, Tilden.
———. County Clerk's Office, Medina County, Hondo.
———. County Clerk's Office, Uvalde County, Uvalde.
DeMontel, Charles. Papers. Barker Texas History Center, University of Texas at Austin.
DeMontel File. James Menke Collection, San Antonio.
Diocesan Records. Diocese of Galveston-Houston, Houston.
Election Registers. Secretary of State Records. Archives, Texas State Library, Austin.
Executive Record Book, 1846–47. Archives, Texas State Library, Austin.
Fitzsimon Papers. Amarillo Public Library, Amarillo.
Fretelliere, August. "Adventures d'un Castrovillain." August Fretelliere Papers, Barker Texas History Center, University of Texas at Austin.
General Land Office of Texas. Files of Original Land Owners. Austin.
Gentilz, Theodore. "Voyage a'la Laguna San Miguel, Texas; November 2, 1847." Gentilz-Fretelliere Papers, Daughters of the Republic of Texas Library, San Antonio.
Haass, H. E. Papers. Barker Texas History Center, University of Texas at Austin.
———. Papers. Texas Collection, Baylor University, Waco.
Habe File. James Menke Collection, San Antonio.
Huffman File. James Menke Collection, San Antonio.
Huth, Ferdinand Louis. Papers, Barker Texas History Center, University of Texas at Austin.
Ihnken File. James Menke Collection, San Antonio.
Lafitte, Jacques. "Le Emprunt." Henri Castro Papers, Barker Texas History Center, University of Texas at Austin.
Leinweber File. James Menke Collection, San Antonio.
Memorials and Petitions. Archives, Texas State Library, Austin.
Muster Rolls. Archives, Texas State Library, Austin.
Nickel, Helen Marie, and Patsy Schurchart. "The Christopher Schurchart Family," Schurchart File, James Menke Collection, San Antonio.
Odin, Jean Marie. Journal, 1842–43. Typescript. Diocesan Records, Diocese of Galveston-Houston, Houston.

————. Papers. Diocesan Records, Diocese of Galveston-Houston, Houston.

————. Papers. Catholic Archives of Texas, Austin.

Parish Register. St. Dominic's Catholic Church, Dhanis.

Parish Register. St. Louis Catholic Church, Castroville.

Poehler File. James Menke Collection, San Antonio.

Redus, Sally. "The Life of Mrs. John Redus," Redus File, James Menke Collection, San Antonio.

Rothe File. James Menke Collection, San Antonio.

Schurchart File. James Menke Collection, San Antonio.

Siever File. James Menke Collection, San Antonio.

Société de Colonisation Europée-Américain au Texas. "Avis au Immigrants s'embarquens au Havre," Ben R. Franklin File, James Menke Collection, San Antonio.

Sumpter, Jesse. "Life of Jesse Sumpter, the Oldest Living Citizen of Eagle Pass, Texas (1902)." Barker Texas History Center, University of Texas at Austin.

Texas. Department of State Copybooks of Diplomatic Correspondence, 1836–46. Archives, Texas State Library, Austin.

Texas. Secretary of State Records. Archives, Texas State Library, Austin.

U.S. Department of Commerce, Bureau of the Census. Seventh Census of the United States, 1850: Schedule I, Free Inhabitants.

————. Bureau of the Census. Seventh Census of the United States, 1850: Schedule II, Slaves.

————. Bureau of the Census. Seventh Census of the United States, 1850: Schedule IV, Agriculture.

————. Bureau of the Census. Eighth Census of the United States, 1860: Schedule I, Free Inhabitants.

————. Bureau of the Census. Eighth Census of the United States, 1860: Schedule II, Slaves.

————. Bureau of the Census. Eighth Census of the United States, 1860: Schedule III, Agriculture.

Vance, Frank Y. Papers, St. Mary's University, San Antonio.

Weimers File. James Menke Collection, San Antonio.

Wipff File. James Menke Collection, San Antonio.

Wurzbach File. James Menke Collection, San Antonio.

Newspapers

Antwerp (Belgium) *Precursor*, 1846.

Austin *National Register*, 1844–45.

Austin *Texas Democrat*, 1846–47.
Austin *Texas Sentinel*, 1841.
Austin *Texas State Gazette*, 1849–60.
Castroville *Anvil*, 1897.
Colmar (Germany) *Courrier d'Alsace*, 1846.
Colmar (Germany) *Diskalia*, 1846.
Corpus Christi Gazette, 1846.
Galveston *Civilian and Galveston Gazette*, 1844–51.
Galveston News, 1846–47.
Galveston *Weekly Journal*, 1851.
Hondo *Anvil-Herald*, 1946–78.
Houston *Telegraph and Texas Register*, 1837–47.
Lacoste Ledger, 1922.
Lagrange *Intelligencer*, 1844.
Ozona *Kicker*, 1927.
San Antonio *Express*, 1924–27.
San Antonio *Ledger*, 1858.
San Antonio *Light*, 1935.
San Antonio *Southern Messenger*, 1895.
San Antonio *Texas Sun*, 1880.
San Antonio *Western Texan*, 1850.

Published Works

Adams, Ephraim Douglass, ed. *British Diplomatic Correspondence Concerning the Republic of Texas*. Austin: Texas State Historical Association, 1917.
Appendix to the Journals of the House of Representatives of the Republic of Texas, Fifth Congress.
Barker, Nancy Nichols, ed. *The French Legation in Texas*. 2 vols. Austin: Texas State Historical Association, 1973.
Bass, Feris A. and B. R. Brunson, eds. *Fragile Empires: The Texas Correspondence of Samuel Swartwout and James Morgan, 1836–1856*. Austin: Shoal Creek Publishers, 1978.
Bollaert, William. *William Bollaert's Texas*. Edited by W. Eugene Hollon and Ruth Lapham Butler. Norman: University of Oklahoma Press, 1956.
Bracht, Victor. *Texas in 1848*. Translated by Charles Frank Schmidt. 1848; reprinted San Antonio, Texas: Naylor, 1931.
Castro, Henri. *Memorial of Henry Castro, Founder of Castro's Colony to the Senate and House of Representatives of the State of Texas*. San Antonio: Ledger, 1855.
Castro, Lorenzo. *Immigration from Alsace-Lorraine: A Brief Sketch of*

Henry Castro's Colony in Western Texas. San Antonio: Herald Office, 1871.

Connor, Seymour V., ed. *Texas Treasury Papers*. 4 vols. Austin: Texas State Library, 1955.

Domenech, Abbe Emmanuel. *Missionary Adventures in Texas and Mexico, A Personal Narrative of Six Years' Sojourn in Those Regions*. Translator unknown. London: Longman, Brown, Green, Longmans, and Roberts, 1858.

Gammel, H. P. N. *The Laws of Texas, 1822–1897*. Austin: 1898.

Garrison, George P., ed. *Diplomatic Correspondence of the Republic of Texas*. 3 vols. Washington, D.C.: Government Printing Office, 1911.

General Land Office of Texas. *Abstract of All Original Texas Land Titles Comprising Grants and Locations to August 31, 1941*. 7 vols. Austin: General Land Office of Texas. 1941.

Jones, Anson. *Memoranda and Official Correspondence Relating to the Republic of Texas, Its History and Annexation*. 1859; reprinted Chicago: Rio Grande Press, 1966.

Journal of the House of Representatives of the Republic of Texas, Fifth Congress, First Session.

Kennedy, William. *Texas: The Rise, Progress, and Prospects of the Republic of Texas*. 1841; reprinted Clifton, New Jersey: Augustus M. Kelley, 1974.

Latham, Francis S. *Travels in the Republic of Texas, 1842*. Gerald S. Pierce, ed. Austin: Encino Press, 1971.

The Life and Diary of Reading W. Black. Uvalde, Texas: El Progresso Club, 1934.

Meusbach, John O. *Answer to Interrogatories*. 1894; reprinted Austin: Pemberton Press, 1964.

Military Law of Texas, An Act to Perfect the Organization of State Troops. Austin: Standard, 1862.

Olmsted, Frederick Law. *A Journey Through Texas*. New York: Dix, Edwards, 1857.

Parisot, Pierre Fourier. *The Reminiscences of a Texas Missionary*. San Antonio: Johnson Bros., 1899.

Rankin, Melinda. *Texas in 1850*. Boston: Damrell and Moore, 1850.

Reid, John C. *Reid's Tramp*. 1858; reprinted Austin: Steck, 1935.

Report of the Adjutant General of the State of Texas, June 24, 1870, to December 31, 1870. Austin: Standard, 1870.

Roemer, Ferdinand. *Texas*. Translated by Oswald Mueller. San Antonio: Standard, 1935.

Santleben, August. *A Texas Pioneer*. New York: Neale, 1910.

Seele, Herman. *The Cypress and Other Writings of a German Pioneer in Texas.* Translated by Edward C. Breitenkamp. Austin: University of Texas Press, 1979.

Senate Journal of the Republic of Texas, Fifth Congress, First Session.

Senate Journal of the Republic of Texas, Sixth Congress.

Smither, Harriett. *Journals of the Sixth Congress of the Republic of Texas.* 2 vols. Austin: Steck, 1944.

Solms-Braunfels, Carl. *Texas, 1844–1845.* Translator unknown. Houston: Anson Jones Press, 1936.

Tetzoff, Otto W., ed. and trans. *The Emigrant to Texas.* 1846; reprinted Burnet, Texas: Eakin Publications, 1979.

The War of the Rebellion: A Compilation of the Official Records of the Union and Confederate Armies. 78 vols. Washington, D.C.: Government Printing Office, 1880–1901.

Williams, Amelia W. and Eugene C. Barker, eds. *The Writings of Sam Houston.* 8 vols. Austin: University of Texas Press, 1938–1943.

Williams, R. H. *With the Border Ruffians.* Toronto: Musson, 1919.

Winkler, Ernest W., ed. *Journal of the Secession Convention of Texas, 1861.* Austin: Texas State Library, 1912.

————, ed. *Manuscript Letters and Documents of Early Texians.* Austin: Steck, 1937.

————, ed. *Platforms of Political Parties in Texas.* Austin: Texas State Library, 1916.

Wurzbach, Emil Frederick. *Life and Memoirs of Emil Frederick Wurzbach.* Translated by Franz J. Dohman. San Antonio: Yanaguana Society, 1937.

Secondary Material

Books

Barker, Eugene C. *The Life of Stephen F. Austin, Founder of Texas, 1793–1836.* Austin: Texas State Historical Association, 1949.

Benjamin, Gilbert Giddings. *The Germans in Texas.* New York: Appleton, 1910.

Biesele, Rudolph Leopold. *The History of German Settlements in Texas.* Austin: Von Boeckmann–Jones, 1930.

Binkley, William C. *The Expansionist Movement in Texas.* Berkeley: University of California Press, 1925.

Briggs, G. A. *The Life of Elisha Andrews Briggs.* San Antonio: privately published, 1932.

Brown, John Henry. *History of Texas.* 2 vols. St. Louis; L. E. Daniell, 1892.

———. *Indian Wars and Pioneers of Texas*. St. Louis: L. E. Daniell, 189(?).

Burnham, Walter Dean, *Presidential Ballots, 1836–1892*. Baltimore: Johns Hopkins, 1955.

Calhoun County Historical Survey Committee. *Indianola Scrapbook*. Austin: San Felipe Press, 1974.

Callahan, Sister Mary Generosa, C. D. P. *The History of the Sisters of Divine Providence*. Milwaukee: Bruce Press, 1955.

Catton, Bruce. *The Coming Fury*. New York: Doubleday, 1961.

Chase, Mary Katherine. *Négociations de la Republique du Texas en Europe*. Paris: Librairie Ancienne Honore Champion, 1932.

Cohen, Henry. "Early Jewish Settlements in Texas," in *One Hundred Years of Jewry in Texas*. Dallas: Cokesbury, 1936.

Connor, Seymour V. *The Peters Colony of Texas*. Austin: Texas State Historical Association, 1954.

Considerant, Victor Prosper. *European Colonization in Texas*. New York: Baker, Godwin, 1855.

Craven, Frank Wesley. *The Colonies in Transition*. New York: Harper and Row, 1968.

Dittmar, Glenn W., and Jack W. Stevens. *Soil Survey of Atascosa County, Texas*. Washington, D.C.: Government Printing Office, 1977.

Dittmar, Glenn W.; Michael L. Deike; and Davie L. Richmond. *Soil Survey of Medina County, Texas*. Washington, D.C.: Government Printing Office, 1972.

Fitzmorris, Mary Angela. *Four Decades of Catholicism in Texas, 1820–1860*. Washington, D.C.: Catholic University of America, 1926.

Finger, Josie R. *125th Anniversary of St. Dominic's Catholic Church at Old D'Hanis, Texas*. Hondo, Texas: privately published, 1972.

Gaylord, Warren Harris. *The Sword Was Their Passport*. Baton Rouge: Louisiana State University Press, 1943.

Geue, Chester, and Ethel Hander Geue. *A New Land Beckoned*. Baltimore: Genealogical Publishing, 1982.

Geue, Ethel Hander. *New Homes in a New Land*. Baltimore: Genealogical Publishing, 1982.

Gibson, Charles. *Spain in America*. New York: Harper and Row, 1966.

Gouge, William M. *The Fiscal History of Texas*. Philadelphia: Lippincott, Grambo, 1852.

Haas, Oscar. *History of New Braunfels and Comal County, 1844–1846*. Austin: Steck, 1968.

Handlin, Oscar. *The Uprooted*. New York: Atlantic Monthly Press, 1972.

Hatcher, Mattie Austin. *The Opening of Texas to Foreign Settlement, 1801–1820*. University Bulletin 2714. Austin: University of Texas Press, 1927.

Hogan, William Ransom. *The Texas Republic*. 1946; reprinted Austin: University of Texas Press, 1975.

Hunter, John Marvin. *One Hundred Years in Bandera, 1853–1953*. Bandera, Texas: privately published, 1953.

———. *The Trail Drivers of Texas*. 2 vols. 1920–23; reprinted New York: Argosy-Antiquarian, 1963.

Jacks, L. V. *Claude Dubuis: Bishop of Galveston*. St. Louis: B. Harder Book, 1946.

Jackson, Ronald Vern; Gary Ronald Peeples; and David Schaefermeyer. *Texas 1850 Census Index*. Bountiful, Utah: Accelerated Indexing Systems, 1976.

James, Vinton Lee. *Frontier and Pioneer Recollections of Early Days in San Antonio and West Texas*. San Antonio: Artes Graphics, 1938.

Johnson, Elmer H. *The Natural Regions of Texas*. Austin: University of Texas Press, 1931.

Jordan, Terry G. *German Seed in Texas Soil*. Austin: University of Texas Press, 1975.

———. *Texas Log Buildings: A Folk Architecture*. Austin: University of Texas Press, 1978.

Kendall, Dorothy Steinbomer. *Gentilz: Artist of the Old Southwest*. Austin: University of Texas Press, 1974.

Lang, A. S. *Financial History of the Public Lands in Texas*. Waco: Baylor University Press, 1932.

Lawler, Ruth Curry. *The Story of Castroville*. Castroville: privately published, 1974.

Lest We Forget: Centennial Celebration of the Bethlehem Lutheran Church: Quihi, Texas: 12 October 1952.

Malsch, Brownson. *Indianola: The Mother of Western Texas*. Austin: Shoal Creek, 1977.

McGrath, Sister Paul. *Political Nativism in Texas, 1825–1860*. Washington, D.C.: Catholic University of America, 1930.

Miller, E. T. *A Financial History of Texas*. Austin: University of Texas Press, 1916.

Miller, Thomas Lloyd. *The Public Lands of Texas*. Norman: University of Oklahoma Press, 1972.

Nixon, Pat Ireland. *A Century of Medicine in San Antonio, Texas*. San Antonio: privately published, 1936.

Notestein, Wallace. *The English People on the Eve of Colonization.* New York: Harper and Row, 1954.

125th Anniversary of the Bethlehem Lutheran Church: Quihi, Texas, 1852–1877.

Perrichon, Abbe Jean. *Vie de Monseigneau Dubuis, l'Aporte du Texas.* Lyon, France: privately published, 1900.

Phelan, Macum. *A History of Early Methodism in Texas.* Dallas: Cokesbury, 1924.

Ross, Terri. "Alsatian Architecture in Medina County." In *Built in Texas.* Francis Edward Abernethy, ed. Waco: Texas Folklore Society, 1979.

Sowell, Andrew Jackson. *Early Settlers and Indian Fighters of Southwest Texas.* Austin: Ben C. Jones, 1900.

Stevens, Jack W., and Davie L. Richmond. *Soil Survey of Uvalde County, Texas.* Washington, D.C.: Government Printing Office, 1969.

Streeter, Thomas W. *Bibliography of Texas, 1795–1845.* 3 vols. Cambridge: Harvard University Press, 1960.

Taylor, F. B. and Richmond, Davie L. *Soil Survey of Bexar County, Texas.* Washington, D.C.: Government Printing Office, 1962.

Tiling, Moritz. *History of the German Element in Texas from 1820–1850.* Houston: Rein and Sons, 1913.

Waugh, Julia Nott. *Castroville and Henry Castro, Empresario.* San Antonio, Texas: Standard, 1934.

Webb, Walter Prescott, ed. *Handbook of Texas.* 2 vols. Austin: Texas State Historical Association, 1952.

Williams, Elgin. *The Animating Pursuits of Speculation.* New York: Columbia University Press, 1949.

Wooten, Dudley, ed. *A Comprehensive History of Texas.* Dallas: 1898.

Yoakum, Henderson K. *History of Texas from Its First Settlement in 1685 to Its Annexation to the United States in 1846.* New York: 1858.

Articles

Barker, Eugene C. "Land Speculation as a Cause of the Texas Revolution." *Southwestern Historical Quarterly* 10 (1906): 76–95.

Barker, Nancy N. "Devious Diplomat: Dubois de Saligny and the Republic of Texas." *Southwestern Historical Quarterly* 72 (January 1969): 324–34.

Callahan, Sister M. Generosa. "Henri Castro and James Hamilton." *Southwestern Historical Quarterly* 69 (October, 1965): 174–85.

Cohen, Henry. "Henry Castro: Pioneer and Colonizer." *Publications of the American Jewish Historical Society*, no. 5, 1896.

Connor, Seymour V. "Land Speculation in Texas." *Southwest Review*, Spring, 1954, 138–43.

Crook, Cornelia and Garland Crook. "Fort Lincoln Texas." *Texas Military History* 4: 145–161.

Denton, Bernice Barrett. "Count Alphonso de Saligny and the Franco-Texienne Bill." *Southwestern Historical Quarterly* 45 (October, 1941): 136–46.

Dunn, Roy Sylvan. "The KGB in Texas, 1860–1861." *Southwestern Historical Quarterly* 70 (April, 1967): 543–73.

Faulk, Odie B. "The Penetration of Foreigners and Foreign Ideas into Spanish East Texas, 1793–1810." *East Texas Historical Journal* 2 (1964): 87–94.

Haass, Herman E. "A Brief History of Castro's Colony." *Southwestern Historical Quarterly* 12 (July, 1908): 80.

Henderson, Mary Virginia. "Minor Empresario Contracts for the Colonization of Texas." *Southwestern Historical Quarterly* 31 (1927): 295–324; 32 (1928): 1–28.

"History of Some German Families and Their Part in the Development and Colonization of Texas: Three Generations of Huths." *Texas Centennial Magazine*, March, 1936,

Murray, Myrtle. "Home Life on Early Ranches of Southwest Texas." *The Cattleman* 12, no. 3 (Aug., 1938): 19–21.

Parry, Albert. "An American Empire Builder." *The American Hebrew*, November 16, 1928, unnumbered pages.

Rothe, Josie Marie. "Biography of Heinrich and Emilia Rothe Family." *The Palms* (St. Mary's University) May, 1936, 1–3.

———. "Quihi, Born Amidst the Turbulence of Old Times, is at Peace Today." *San Antonio Light* (San Antonio, Texas), January 13, 1935.

Saathoff, W. N. "Quihi, Settled 105 Years Ago." Anvil Herald (Hondo, Texas), July 22, 1949.

Smyrl, Frank H. "Unionism in Texas, 1856–1861." *Southwestern Historical Quarterly* 68 (October, 1964), 172–95.

"Texas Letters and Documents." *Texana* 6, no. 4 (Winter, 1966): 358.

Wooster, Ralph A. "An Analysis of the Membership of the Texas Secession Convention." *Southwestern Historical Quarterly* 70 (January, 1967). 328–32.

———. "An Analysis of the Texas Know-Nothings." *Southwestern Historical Quarterly* 70 (January, 1967), 414–23.

———. "Foreigners in the Principal Towns of Antebellum Texas." *Southwestern Historical Quarterly* 66 (October, 1962), 208–20.

Theses and Dissertations

Crook, Carland Elaine. "San Antonio, Texas, 1846–1861." Master's thesis, Rice University, 1964.

Gittinger, Theodore G. "A History of St. Louis Catholic Church of Castroville, Texas." Master's thesis, Sam Houston State University, 1972.

Goldthorp, Audrey. "Castro's Colony." Master's thesis, University of Texas, 1928.

Holden, W. C. "Frontier Problems and Movements in West Texas, 1846–1900." Ph.D. dissertation, University of Texas, 1928.

Holsworthy, Sister Mary Xavier. "History of the Diocese of Corpus Christi, Texas." Master's thesis, St. Mary's University, 1948.

Loving, Solon Ollie. "A History of the Fisher-Miller Land Grant from 1842–1860." Master's thesis, University of Texas, 1934.

Paulus, Marjorie. "Fifteen Years in Old San Antonio: 1850–1865." Master's thesis. St. Mary's University, 1939.

Peevy, Lucien Elliot. "The First Two Years of Texas Statehood, 1846–1847." Ph.D. dissertation, University of Texas, 1948.

Pitts, John Bost III. "Speculation in Headright Land Grants in San Antonio from 1837 to 1842." Master's thesis, Trinity University, 1966.

Rece, Bernardine. "San Antonio: Its Beginnings and Its Development under the Republic." Master's thesis, University of Texas, 1941.

Timmons, Joe T. "Texas on the Road to Secession." Ph.D. dissertation, University of Chicago, 1973.

Maps

General Land Office of Texas. Original Property Ownership Map. Atascosa County.

———. Original Property Ownership Map. Bexar County.

———. Original Property Ownership Map. Frio County.

———. Original Property Ownership Map. LaSalle County.

———. Original Property Ownership Map. McMullen County.

———. Original Property Ownership Map. Medina County.

———. Original Property Ownership Map. Uvalde County.

———. Map of Castro's Colony, ca. 1856.

Index

Aberdeen, Lord, 14
Adelsverein. *See* Society for the Protection of German Immigrants in Texas
agriculture, 102−104
Alamo, The, 33
Alsace, 35, 37, 65, 70, 92−93, 98, 100, 139
Algeria, 35
Antonio, Locmar, 44
Antwerp, Belgium, 35, 64, 67, 68−69, 79
Alberdina (ship), 76
Antwerp Society. *See* Société de Colonisation Europée-Américain au Texas
architecture, 97−98
Atascosa County, 110
Aumont, Father Menetrier, 70
Austin, Texas, 14, 74

Baden (German state), 37, 65
Balcones Escarpment, 112
Bangor (ship), 79
Bank of the United States, 4
Bas Rhin, 36, 38
Basterreche, Jean, 8, 11−12
Bavaria, 126
Beals Colony, 15
Bell, P. H., 130
Bethlehem Lutheran Church, 101
Bexar County, 110, 115, 128
bonds, Republic of Texas, 4, 19
Bourgeois d'Orvanne, Alexandre, 18−19, 21, 27−28, 34, 40−42, 45−46, 48, 71
Bourgeois, Jules, 52, 58−59, 64, 80, 128
Brands, Father John, 76
Bremen, Germany, 78−80

Brinkhoff, Gertrude, 77−78
Brinkhoff, Henry, 77−78
Brown, James, 77
Burnham, David, 77

Camp Verde, 133
Carl Wilhelm (ship), 94
Carlshaven, Texas, 81
Carolan, John M., 115−17
Castro's Colony: compared to others, 137−40; condition of, in 1843, 91−92; contract for, 16, 21; defense of, 110; description of, 112−13; motivation to form, 109−10; political organization of, 127−28; profits from, 83−84, 121−23; size of, 110, 117
Castro, Amelia, 121
Castro, Henri, 5, 12−13, 40−41, 57−63, 70, 75, 85−86, 129; Antwerp partners of, 68−69; biographical data on, 13, 24−25; and Castroville, 44−55; death of, 135; and Dhanis, 81, 83; grant obtained by, 15−16; and Huth, 36−37; lands received by, 117−20; and profits from grant, 121−23; and recruiting in Europe, 23−31
Castro, Lorenzo, 121, 128, 135
Castroville, Texas, 50−54, 60−61, 69, 97, 120
cattle raisers, 125−27
Causici, Angelo, 119, 121, 128
Causici, Mrs., 66
Charobiny, Francesca, 107
Charobiny, Rudolph, 107
Chazelle, Father, 102
Cherokee lands, 19, 41
cholera, 95, 105

155

churches, 51–52, 59, 76, 98–99, 100–101
Civil War, 131–36
coastal plains soils, 112
Colmar, 57, 63, 86
colonists: adaptation of, to Texas lifestyle, 102–108; as cattle raisers, 125–27; changing aspects of, 129; condition of, in 1843, 38, 70–78, 92–93; condition of, in 1844, 42, 74–75; as farmers, 89–90; financial status of, 92–93; first reaction of, to Texas, 32–34; lands received by, 117; motivation of, to emigrate, 92–93; number of, receiving grants, 114–20; numbers of, 96 and n, 109, 112; occupations of, 124–25; perceptions of, of Texas, 48–49; places of origin of, 89, 93–94; qualifications of, 111; recruitment of, 70–71; as sheep raisers, 127; and trip from Europe to Texas, 93–95; as Union sympathizers, 134–36
Comanche Indians, 51, 106
Compagnie Générale de Colonisation au Texas, 41
Confederate army, 134
Copano Bay, 81, 95
Corpus Christi, Texas, 65, 79, 115
Cramayel, Jules de, 63
Crawford, James, 62
Cremavesi, H. and C., Company, 80
Cronstadt (ship), 78
Cunningham, M. F., 62
Cupples, Dr. George, 50, 51, 64, 105

De Cocke and Bischop Company, 64, 66
Demontel, Charles. *See* Montel, Charles de
Dhanis, Guillaume, 68–69, 79, 81, 85
Dhanis, Texas, 81, 83, 98, 100, 104, 107, 113
Domenech, Father Emmanuel, 101
d'Orvanne, Alexandre Bourgeois. *See* Bourgeois d'Orvanne, Alexandre
drought, 104
Dubuis, Father Claude Marie, 98–101
Ducos, Armand, 18–19, 21, 27, 34, 35
Dunquerque, 28, 35

Eagle Pass, Texas, 110
Ebro (ship), 28, 32–33
education, 101–102
Elliot, William, 58, 84
exchequer currency, 4

Fest, Henry, 125
Fest, Simon, 125
financial panic of 1837, 3–4
Fisher, Henry F., 17, 48
Fisher-Miller Grant, 17, 21, 48, 137
Fort Lincoln, 107, 136
Franco-Texienne Bill, 8–11, 13–14, 15, 19
Fredericksburg, Texas, 138–39
French legation building, 14
Frio County, 110, 113
Frio River, 75, 113
frontier defense, 134

Gallinas River, 125
Galveston, Texas, 23, 28, 31–32, 34, 38, 42, 48, 58, 60, 65, 73, 76–77, 80, 87, 93, 115
General Land Office of Texas, 6–7
Gentilz, Theodore, 50, 64, 86
Grossenbacher, Barbara, 104
Grossenbacher, John, 104
Guilbeau, F., 52
Guizot, Pierre François, 25, 34, 35

Haller, August, 54
Haass, Louis, 52, 54, 128, 135
Hamilton, James, 4–5, 9, 12, 13, 17
Hart, Samuel, 62
Haut Rhin, 37, 38, 70, 73
Henrich (ship), 37–38
Holland, 37
Hondo Creek, 45, 113
houses, 55, 58, 97–98
Houston, Sam, 4, 8–9, 12, 14, 18, 25, 33, 43, 91
Houston, Texas, 32, 47
Huffman, Dr. John, 105
Huth, Albert, 65
Huth and Company, 36, 66, 68, 70, 80
Huth, Louis Ferdinand, 36, 38–39, 42, 52, 54, 58–59, 64, 69, 73, 76–77, 79–80, 84, 86, 128
Huth, Ludwig, 36, 66, 85

Illis, John H., 87, 120–21
immigrants. *See* colonists
Indian relations, 105–107
Indianola, Texas, 81, 95, 105

James, John, 44, 51, 52, 80
Jassaud, Jean, 16
Jean Key (ship), 37
Jeanette Marie (ship), 38
Jones, Anson, 10, 13, 17, 30, 43

Kennedy, William, 14–17, 21
Kickapoo Indians, 106–107
Kinney, Henry, 65, 79
Knights of the Golden Circle (K.G.C.), 133–34
Know-Nothing Party, 129–30

LaCoste, J. B., 119
Lafitte, Jacques, 5, 12–13, 16
Lamar, Mirabeau B., 4, 9–10, 11
land commissioners, 115–19
land contracts, 26–27
land grants: Bourgeois-Ducos Grant, 18–19, 21, 27–28, 34; Castro Colony, 16, 109–23; comparison of, 137–40; as First Class Headrights, 6; Fisher-Miller Grant, 17; Kennedy-Pringle Grant, 16–18, 21; McMullen Grant, 46–47, 84; Mexican, 3; as military bonus, 6; Peters Colony Grant, 15; Pirson Grant, 17–18; as Second Class Headrights, 6; Spanish, 3; as Third Class Headrights, 7, 10
land laws, 10
Lanfear, Mr., 42
Laredo, Texas, 110
LaSalle County, Texas, 110
Lassaulx, Pierre, 8, 11, 12
Laude, Albert, 29
Laurent, Claude, 91
Lavaca Bay, 32, 61, 74, 80–81, 91, 95, 115
lawsuits, 57, 63, 120–21, 129
Le Havre, 35
Leingolsheim, Alsace, 71
Lienhard, Father, 74
Lipan Apaches, 77–78, 105–107
lots: in Castroville, 48, 58; in Dhanis, 81; outlots, 47, 55, 58, 75, 80, 83; in Quihi, 75; in Vandenburg, 80
Louis Philippe (ship), 28–29, 38, 70
Lyons (ship), 28

Marne (French department), 35
Martin and Cobb Company, 60, 65
Martin, Elizie, 29
Maverick, Samuel, 119, 130
Mayfield, James, 8
McMullen County, Texas, 110
McMullen Grant, 46–47, 84
McMullen, John, 46–47
McMullen-McGloin Colony, 115
Medina County, Texas, 110, 112, 128, 131, 133
Medina River, 44–45, 50, 104–105
Medio Creek, 54

Menetrier, Mr., 54
Mercier, Mr., 53
Mexican War, 81, 107, 129
Meyer, Blas, 107
Miller, Burchard, 17, 48
Miller, Washington, 43
Montel, Charles de, 50–51, 107, 132, 134
Monterrey, Mexico, 135

Nassau (German state), 37
Nauendorf, A., 132
Neufreystadt, Baden, 36, 80
New Braunfels, Texas, 78, 81, 99, 138–39
New Fountain Methodist Church, 100–101
New Fountain, Texas, 100–101
New Orleans, 40–41, 61, 84, 95
Norvegian (ship), 73–74

Ocean (ship), 37–38
Odin, Bishop Jean Marie, 42, 51, 52, 59, 61, 67, 68, 76, 91, 98
Oefinger, Rev. Christian, 101
Oge, Rev. Jules, 51–52
Ordinance of Secession, 132
Osy, Texas, 113

Parker Creek, 81
Paul, James, 133–34
Pease, E. M., 130
Peters Colony, 10–11, 15, 21, 137–40
Peters, W. S., 10–11
Pfanner, Father Grigiore, 61, 70, 73–76, 84, 98
Phene, François, 29
Pirson, Victor, 12, 14, 17–18
Pleasanton, Texas, 125
pneumonia, 95
Powers, James, 81
Price, W. W., 62
Pringle, William, 16–17
Probus (ship), 70, 73–74, 126
Prussia, 38

Quihi Lake, 45, 54, 62, 64, 75, 77–78
Quihi, Texas, 76–78, 80, 81, 98, 100, 104, 107, 113

red backs, 4
religion, 51–52, 59, 76, 98–101
Rhin, Ziliac, 48, 67, 95
Richarz, H. J., 127
Reicherger, Franck, 134
Riegert, Mr., 71

Robertson, W., 62
Riotte, Charles N., 117, 119
Rothe, August, 127
Rothe family, 126–27
Rothe, Fritz, 127
Rothe, Henry, 127
Rothe, Louis, 127
Roilet, Mr., 55
Rump, Mr., 45, 53

Saint Dominic's Catholic Church,
　101
Saint Louis Catholic Church, 51–52,
　59, 76, 98–99
Saligny, Dubois de, 8–9, 11, 13, 18,
　24–25
San Antonio River, 33
San Antonio, Texas, 28, 33, 42
San Miguel Creek, 113
San Miguel, Texas, 113
Santitas Ranch, 48
Schanunga (ship), 125
Scheidemontle, Charles. *See* Montel,
　Charles de
Seco Creek, 107, 113
sheep raisers, 127
slavery, 131
Sloman, Mr., 80
Smith, Ashbel, 23, 25, 27
Société de Colonisation Europée-
　Américain au Texas in Paris, 26
Société de Colonisation Europée-
　Américain au Texas in Antwerp.,
　68–69, 78–81, 84, 86–87

Society for the Protection of German
　Immigrants in Texas, 41, 48, 78,
　80–81, 137–40
Solms-Braunfels, Prince Carl, 40–42,
　45, 48, 61
southern blacklands belt, 112
Strasbourg, 57, 63, 86
Switzerland, 65, 67–68, 92

Telegraph and Texas Register, 19, 21, 60
Texas National Register, 60
Texas Rangers, 54, 106–107
Trevino, Augustin, 77

Ulrich, Joseph, 119
Union army, 134–36
Uvalde County, Texas, 110
Vandenburg, Texas, 80, 98–100, 104,
　113
Verde Creek, 80, 100, 133
Victoria, Texas, 34, 67, 76, 115

Waelder, Jacob, 130
Wantz family, 125–26
Wantz, Ignatz, 126
Wantz, Xavier, 126
Ward, Tro, 116, 119
Washington, D.C., 12
Washington-on-the-Brazos, 43, 59
Wycale, Thomas, 135

yellow fever, 48

Zion Lutheran Church, 101